NAME _____

ENTERED _____20_____

PASSED _____20_____

RAISED _____20_____

AT

_____

LODGE, NO._____

_____, PA

Also, by Robert E. Burtt

Wait Until Sunset: Memories of a Distant Conflict

Rome: A Commonplace Book

A Guide to Modern Freemasonry

Heart of the Mystery: A Novel

A

Pennsylvania

Masonic

Handbook

The Personal *Ahiman Rezon*

By

Robert E. Burtt

Creare Spazio Editrice

Burtt, Robert E.

A Pennsylvania Masonic Handbook:
The Personal Ahiman Rezon

Includes bibliographical references

ISBN-10: 1456323970
ISBN-13: 978-1456323974

Manufactured in the United States of America

Creare Spazio Editrice

by

Createspace, an Amazon company

Middletown, Delaware 19709

10th Edition, 2022

To

The Brethren of years past,
who laid the foundations of our Order.

To

The Brethren of today,
now charged with continuing the work.

To

The Brethren of tomorrow,
who will dazzle us with cunning workmanship,
and build a structure that will be the wonder of the world.

"As useful knowledge is the great object of our desire, we Ought to apply ourselves with zeal to the practice and profession of Freemasonry. The ways of wisdom are beautiful, and lead to pleasure. Knowledge is attained by degrees, and cannot everywhere be found. Wisdom seeks the secret shade, and the lonely cell, designed for contemplation. There enthroned she sits, delivering her sacred oracles. There we are to seek her, and to pursue the real bliss."[1]

---From the Opening Charge.

[1] Untitled pamphlet distributed by Committee on Masonic Education, Grand Lodge F. & A. M. of Pennsylvania. Authorized and Approved by the Right Worshipful Grand Master. *circa* 1995.

TABLE OF CONTENTS

"In the name of God, and Holy St. John,"

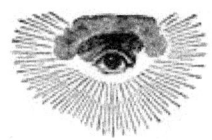

OPENING
What Just Happened?

I was born and raised in Pennsylvania and spent much of my adult life there. I was also "raised" a Master Mason under the auspices of the Grand Lodge of Pennsylvania. Modern life being what it is, I no longer live in the "Keystone State." My career, along with the twists and turns of life, has deposited me in another part of our nation. I still get back home whenever I can however. Always on the agenda is staying with family, getting back in touch with old friends, and—if possible—attending a meeting at my old lodge. Technically, it's simply my *lodge*, not my "old" lodge. I've never transferred my membership. It was during just such a visit that the idea for this book occurred to me.

When I was planning my trip, I read my monthly lodge notice and saw that there was going to be an extra stated meeting, and that two Third Degrees were going to be given. My father and I decided to attend. It was everything I expected it to be. My Brothers were surprised and pleased to see me again. The food was enjoyable (always a key element in a meeting), and the degrees were performed very ably.

Part of the fun of seeing a conferral is the chance to vicariously take part in the degree with the candidate. While I listen to the ritual, I often catch myself daydreaming about past degrees I've seen, or participated in. I sometimes think about my past mistakes, slips of the tongue, mechanical errors, and memory lapses in the ritual—it all comes back.

That's a little-known part of Masonic fun: the charms of memory.

When the ceremony was finished, I went over to the new Master Masons, shook their hands, and welcomed them to our "Ancient and Honorable Order." I saw something that I remembered from my own initiation: a look in their eyes that said: "What just happened to me?" Even though it often takes around five months to petition and join a lodge, that's not enough time for the average man to absorb the whole experience. I've never met a Brother yet who hasn't confessed to being confused, dazed, and almost overwhelmed by his initiation into the Masonic mysteries. On the drive back from lodge, I made the decision to write this book.

The literature of Freemasonry is vast. If you were to read a book on the Craft every day for the rest of your life, you wouldn't begin to make a dent in the published body of work. In recent years, the public's interest in Freemasonry has experienced a revival of sorts. Several films have been released with Masonic themes. A few popular novels that contain Templar history have become best sellers. Masonry also remains a staple on TV and the internet. So, one might ask: why another book? What does this particular work have to offer?

I've explored a good portion of Masonic writing. I don't claim to be an expert, but I think I have some expertise. There are very few books written for the "newly raised" Brother. Some exist, but many are fairly dated, having been published over half a century ago. Something new is needed, and I hope this work can meet that need.

There is also a problem of specificity. Freemasonry not a unified, monolithic whole. It *has* spread over most of the world into almost every nation. Many countries have a single governing body, called a Grand Lodge. These Grand Lodges are responsible for formulating rules and enforcing their authority within that country. There are some exceptions to this rule, one of them being the Masonic structure in the United States. Freemasonry is set up on a state-by-state basis. There are fifty-one Grand Lodges: one for each state, and one for the District of Columbia. Each Grand Lodge, while recognizably Masonic and American, is very different. The ritual, customs, language—even the spirit—are all distinctive. Think of it this way: just as each of our states has its own individual history and story, so do each of the fifty-one Grand Lodges. This situation presents a problem for new Pennsylvania Freemasons however.

Pennsylvania is unique. We are like no other Grand Lodge. If you pick up a book to familiarize yourself with Masonry, it will help you—but only in a general way. Much that pertains to Pennsylvania will not be available. My lodge used to give a book to new members.[2] It contained detailed explanations of many Masonic symbols and ceremonies. However, most were not part of the Pennsylvania ritual. It had drawings illustrating scenes that aren't in our work. With the book was a diagram of a lodge room. It resembled a Pennsylvania lodge only in a general way. A lot was left out. More was added and turned around. I feel that, as members of the Grand Lodge of Pennsylvania, we have our own special needs and require our own "guidebook" to the mysteries.

Finally, I must say that in my opinion, most Masonic literature—while interesting—is not worth the average Brother's time. Much of it is pure speculation, or random musings. Depending on your depth of imagination, one can spend an inordinate amount of time talking and speculating about the symbols of our order. The problem is that it gets

---

[2] Allen E. Roberts, *The Craft and Its Symbols: Opening the Door to Masonic Symbolism,* Richmond, VA: Macoy Publishing and Masonic Supply Company, Inc., 1974. This is considered a classic of its kind. It is a very good book for most Masonic jurisdictions.

old. How many times can you read books that contain one man's theories about the Square and Compasses? After a while, everyone starts to repeat one another. This work aims to give a basic treatment of Masonic symbolism as it pertains to *Pennsylvania*, with a minimum of my personal, private theories.

Now some caveats. This work is my own, and I am solely responsible for any errors, mistakes, and problems contained within it. Also, I speak only for myself—not for my lodge, not for the Grand Lodge of Pennsylvania—and certainly not for Freemasonry in general. Whatever is useful in this book, I owe to the Brethren that have gone before me. Whatever is problematic is my responsibility.[3] I've met some of the best of men during my Masonic journey. I came to Freemasonry as a mature man in early middle age. There was little more I could learn about human nature—I thought. The lodge opened up a whole new area of knowledge and self-exploration to me.

Hopefully, I can help *you*, the newly raised Master Mason, by pointing out some shortcuts and interesting paths for you to explore in this, your new life. This book can be read from beginning to end, or you can simply pick it up at random and read about separate topics. It is my hope that this little work will help you start to answer that question: *"What just happened?"*

---

[3] This is a good place to thank the late Brother Thomas W. Jackson, Past Right Worshipful Grand Secretary of the Grand Lodge of Pennsylvania, who provided me with an insightful series of observations that improved and refined this work. I am indebted to him for his wisdom, and experience. I would also like to express my undying appreciation to the late Brother James F. Standish Jr., then Secretary of the Pennsylvania Lodge of Research, for his unfailing support and belief in this book and in me. I look forward to our meeting in that celestial lodge above, "that house not made with hands, eternal in the heavens!"

The Keystone.
One of the symbols of the Commonwealth of
Pennsylvania. Also important in Masonic Symbolism.

Pennsylvania Facts

The first Masonic lodges in Pennsylvania met in local taverns. One of the first recorded meetings took place in Philadelphia in an establishment called The Tun Tavern. This was also where the Grand Lodge met. Tun Tavern is, at the present time, being restored and reconstructed. In 1775, The Continental Navy advertised for recruits for a "Corps of Marines" there, thus making the Tun Tavern the birthplace not only of The Grand Lodge of Pennsylvania, but also of the United States Marine Corps.

On July 3, 1863, Confederate troops under General Lewis Armistead attacked Federal positions on Cemetery Hill at the Battle of Gettysburg. As he lay mortally wounded, Armistead was comforted by a young Union lieutenant named Frank Haskell. He gave him water and saw to his personal effects. Both Armistead and Haskell were Freemasons. A battlefield monument commemorates this event.

PART I

TAKE A STEP FORWARD:

THE LODGE

(Overleaf) With the flap turned up, the apron of an Entered Apprentice Mason.

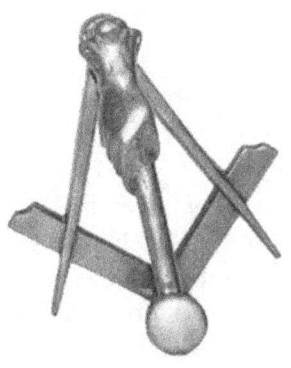

1. WELCOME TO FREEMASONRY!

Welcome my Brother. Welcome to our "Most Ancient and Honorable Fraternity." It's good to have you with us. You are now a member of one of the most fascinating organizations in the world. If one stops to think about it, there are only three modern entities that have world-wide pretensions: the Roman Catholic Church, the United Nations, and Freemasonry. Each of these institutions has branches in almost every country on the globe. Each has an all-encompassing, unifying, peaceful, goal for humanity. All have long, proud histories. As a Freemason, you now have certain rights, privileges, and obligations. Your first obligation is to understand a little about the history of this, our ancient Order.

The story of Freemasonry is complicated for several reasons. First, the records of the Brotherhood have been lost and scattered over the centuries. Second, Freemasons have, for the most part, been a secretive group, keeping aloof from the outside world, and hiding their institutional knowledge. And lastly, Masons have succeeded in confusing even themselves, conjuring up wild theories and stories about our origins. Until recently, most of us have been left to grasp at mythology, half-baked history, and outright fabrications to explain our story. In recent years, the historical profession has done an outstanding job of tracing the roots of Freemasonry and backing up their findings with hard, academically respectable, proof.

We know that Freemasonry had its public beginning on June 24, 1717, St. John the Baptist's Day, in London, England. On that day, four city lodges met at the Goose and Gridiron Ale House and formed the Grand Lodge of England. Anthony Sayer, Gentleman, was chosen Grand Master, along with a slate of lesser officers. It is from this date that most modern histories of Freemasonry begin.[4] This fact alone is pretty impressive. How many groups have achieved, and then passed, their three hundredth birthday? There is an obvious question, however. If Masonry began on this date, where did the four lodges come from? They had to have already been in existence. They didn't just appear out of thin air!

Traditionally, Masonic writers have spun various theories about the Craft's origins that trace our starting point back to several ancient—and sometimes glamorous beginnings.

Some argue that our origins are found in the medieval stone mason's guilds. Others have claimed that Freemasons are the lineal descendants of the Order of Knights Templar, dating back to the Crusades. Finally, many early "scholars" of the Craft have fallen back on a literal reading of the ritual, arguing that our beginning dates to King Solomon's building of the Temple at Jerusalem. The vast majority of such writings have very little in the way of proof to recommend them. Hard facts are generally nonexistent. Scholarship of recent years has been much more rigorous. Evidence found by current researchers paints

---

[4] Henry Wilson Coil, *A Comprehensive View of Freemasonry,* Richmond, VA: Macoy Publishing & Masonic Supply Co., Inc.,1998. pp. 69-71.

a much more nuanced picture, and advances a more sophisticated set of explanations for the birth, and emergence in 1717, of Masonry.

One must remember that the modern world, as we know it, is relatively young. What I mean by that is that the major pillars of western civilization are much newer and more fragile than we like to admit. Freedom of thought, association, and religion, did not exist in a way we would recognize just a couple of hundred years ago. For that matter, come to think of it, much of the world even *today* does not subscribe to the values of individualism and freedom. Another thing that we moderns tend to forget is that human progress is not always simple, straightforward, or even inevitable. Living in a "First World" country, it is easy to forget that most of the rest of the world lives and believes, much differently than we do.

In school most of us learned that, after the fall of the Roman Empire, there was a period of barbarism, followed by the Middle Ages, the Renaissance, the Enlightenment, and finally, the Modern World that we live in today. Everything is nice, tidy, and neat. No problems, no detours, one step leads to another, on and on, ending in the modern world that we enjoy now. Sorry, but that's not the way history happened.

It *is* true that the Renaissance saw an explosion of human progress in almost every field imaginable. Much Greek and Roman literature was rediscovered in forgotten libraries and monasteries. The system of higher education that we know today was invented in Italy and France. Art—especially painting and sculpture—leapt ahead and has seldom been equaled since. The beginning of what we now call "The Scientific Method" also began to take shape in the Western mind.

Science, however, is a tricky business. It always has been. Its basic goal is to explain the world—all of it. At issue is the fact that man has always had problems reorienting his explanation of reality. Thinking is hard. Changing ones' mind is painful. Who among us finds it exhilarating to find that our basic assumptions and beliefs need to be reexamined? Now extrapolate that feeling to a society. Human institutions become vested in viewing the world in a certain way. If anyone, or any movement, comes along to challenge those assumptions, it is viewed as a threat. And threats to the established order need to be crushed.[5] Socrates was one of the first figures in Western history to find out about this process. He was put to death for raising basic questions about truth, justice, and the "way things are." The technical charge was teaching the young to not respect the Gods. A quick trial, and a nice drink of hemlock solved this thorny problem for Athens. The process of discovery went on however.

Before we start feeling too superior, we might want to look at the United States today. Think about issues such as the teaching of evolution, prayer in public schools, birth control, full civil rights for gay citizens, racial equality, and all of the legal and constitutional issues associated with the "war on terror." Every society has its blind spots and vested interests. Progress is not a smooth, easy road. Within this uncomfortable fact we find the birth of Freemasonry.

During the Renaissance, modern science was born. Man started to examine the natural world, and explain it without the aid of superstition, dogma, and authoritarian political power. Nicholas Copernicus advanced the idea that the sun was the center of the universe and that the planets revolved around it. Galileo built on this principle by making

---

[5] See Thomas S. Kuhn, *The Structure of Scientific Revolutions*, Chicago, IL: The University of Chicago Press, 1970. Not a great book, but it does explore some of the problems when new scientific theories are advanced in cultures.

observations with a telescope and started amassing empirical evidence to support the Copernican theory of the universe. All well and good, you might suppose; and you would suppose wrongly. The Roman Catholic Church had several hundred years of intellectual work invested in the Aristotelian Theory of the universe which stated that the *earth*, not the sun, was its center. Religious authority became wedded to this view, along with political considerations. To make an extremely long story short, Galileo was hauled before the Holy Inquisition and made to publicly recant his beliefs about the earth revolving around the sun. He spent the rest of his life under house arrest. Recently, the Vatican has admitted that "mistakes were made" in this affair.[6] Before you jump to conclusions, it must be pointed out that no one church had a monopoly on intolerance. Martin Luther's view of the Copernican theory was almost exactly the same as the Vatican's. And his solution to dissent was similar as well.

To be interested in science during the Renaissance was literally playing with fire. Galileo barely escaped being burnt at the stake. A fellow Italian, named Giordano Bruno, was not so lucky. Bruno was a multi-talented philosopher, scientist, and theologian whose life illustrates the problems one could run into exploring the scientific world in this period. In 1600 he ended up being burnt at the stake in Rome by the Inquisition. Bruno was interested in everything from chemistry to astronomy, also theology, and what we now call psychology. And there lies the danger. After several hundred years, The Scientific Method has had a lot of time to separate "good" science, from "bad" science. At

---

6 Alan Cowell, "After 350 Years, Vatican Says Galileo was Right: It Moves," *The New York Times*, October 31, 1992, p. A-1.

the beginning of the process, it was impossible for even some of the greatest intellects to figure out what was what.

Today, we think of Sir Isaac Newton as the great thinker who invented calculus, discovered the laws of motion and gravity, and who studied the spectrum of light. All true. What is not so well known is that he spent the last third of his life looking for hidden messages in the Bible so that he could predict the future as well as trying to figure out how to turn base metals into gold.[7] It's not that the line between magic, the occult, and science was blurred during this time, the line actually didn't exist! If you're inventing science, you try everything, because how do you know something isn't valid until it's been proven *not* to work?

It was this type of thinking that got Giordano Bruno into trouble with the Roman Catholic Church. If astronomical observations can provide data so that the movements of the heavenly bodies can be predicted, how do we know that the stars don't affect us here on earth? We now know (most of us) that astrology doesn't work. We also know that the Bible can't be used to predict the stock market. It took a long time for humans to figure out the divide between science and superstition. Bruno and his fellow thinkers were convinced that there was a hidden, underlying power in the universe that controlled everything. If man could discover this power, there would be no limit to what he could do here on earth.[8] In order to explore these exciting ideas, philosophers and students formed private *academies*, where like-minded thinkers could discuss, explore, and argue about new ideas and paradigms. New discoveries could also be presented. These academies were

---

[7] Francis A. Yates, *The Rosicrucian Enlightenment,* New York, NY: Routledge, 1972. pp. 204-05.

[8] We now know that this "hidden power" is mathematics, but many of the Renaissance thinkers had something magical in mind.

temporary, *ad hoc* gatherings, sort of like discussion groups, or seminars. They started in Rome, but gradually spread to most major cities in Europe. Few lasted very long, and most were centered around one outstanding thinker, who organized the group. All were by invitation only. All were very, very private, for reasons that must be obvious by now. Whether you were in Rome, or London, or Germany, it didn't pay to advertise the fact that you and your friends were dabbling in science and philosophy.

Sorry this took so long. So now let's get back to our friend Giordano Bruno. As I've said, he led an interesting, exciting, and dangerous life, constantly moving from place to place, trying to propagate his ideas. Born near Naples, Italy, he lived in Rome, Venice, Germany, Paris, and—what is interesting to Freemasons—in London from 1583 to 1585.[9] There he was a sensation, publishing a major scientific work, lecturing, arguing, and, incidentally, forming an academy to help spread his world-views. His ideas of mysticism, hidden knowledge, and new learning spread through Elizabethan England. One influential enthusiast was William Schaw, Master of the Kings Works in Scotland.[10] Historians of Scottish Freemasonry have proven that Schaw played *the* major role in transforming Scottish stone craft guilds of workingmen into early forms of Masonic lodges.[11] Associations of stoneworkers provided a perfect "cover" for scholars and thinkers to meet and discuss the "New Learning." Freemasonry, as we know it, started in Scotland. Soon its' ideas spread to England and took root among the already existing medieval guilds.

---

[9] Francis A. Yates, *The Art of Memory*, Chicago, IL: The University of Chicago Press, 1966. pp. 199-204.

[10] Coil, p. 54.

[11] David Stevenson, *The Origins of Freemasonry,* Cambridge: Cambridge University Press, 1998.

Through the 1600's there are scattered references to Freemasonry in diaries, a few surviving lodge records, and in newspapers—particularly late in the century. During this period, the makeup of membership in Masonic lodges changed. Previously, lodges had been composed of stonemasons and laborers. Now membership began to consist of men with no connection to the building trades. The movement grew steadily and gathered strength until it burst into public view in 1717 in London.

Freemasonry really came into its own during the 1700's, a period known as "The Enlightenment." The orientation of the Craft had also changed. Where before it had attracted scientists, mathematicians, or those interested in research, now it appealed to laymen with philosophic and political interests. The agenda of Freemasonry became revolutionary—for its time. England in the 1700's was a class-based society, with the monarch on top, then the aristocracy, and commoners at the bottom. Slaves, women, and those who did not subscribe to the Anglican faith, were non-persons. The Masonic Lodge offered an alternative society. Each lodge had a set of rules and regulations that members swore to uphold. Each member was equal to all other members within the confines of the lodge. The leadership was elected by all the members and their powers were restricted by the constitution of that lodge. Every lodge was thus a mini-republic in a society that was ruled by force and privilege. This was a radical way of looking at the world for the time. Police arrest records have been unearthed in Paris from the 1740's which accuse Freemasons of subverting the state by engaging in these "republican" activities.[12]

---

[12] Margaret C. Jacob, *Living the Enlightenment: Freemasonry and Politics in Eighteenth-Century Europe*, Oxford: Oxford University Press, 1991. pp. 3-8.

The Masonic movement swept through Europe in the first half of the 1700's. Citizens in every country embraced Freemasonry, and almost every governing authority looked with suspicion on the new phenomenon.[13] Freemasonry, since it was of British origin, naturally followed the flag and spread through the British Empire where it made its way to North America and to the Thirteen Colonies. Pennsylvania has the honor to be the third oldest grand lodge in the world. Only the Grand Lodges of England, and of Ireland predate it.[14] I will cover the history of Freemasonry in Pennsylvania in much more detail in another chapter.

Freemasonry has had a varied reputation, and its influence has waxed and waned since the Eighteenth Century. In certain times, Freemasonry has been used to support the established political order. In the 1780's, Emperor Joseph II of Austria used Masonic lodges as an element in his attempts to reform church and society within his kingdom.[15] Frederick the Great of Prussia had the same agenda and used Masonic lodges as a virtual arm of the state. In the Nineteenth Century, the Brotherhood was often used by reformers and revolutionary movements to advance their goals. Garibaldi was a committed member and used his Masonic contacts in South America and Italy in his fight to help create the modern nation of Italy in 1860.[16]

---

[13] Ibid.

[14] Wayne A. Huss, *The Master Builders: A History of the Grand Lodge of Free and Accepted Masons of Pennsylvania, Volume I: 1731-1873,* Philadelphia, PA: Grand Lodge, F. & A.M. of Pennsylvania, 1986. p. 19. This is a cause for local pride. Although Massachusetts has long claimed precedence, the latest scholarship gives the laurel to the Keystone state. While very important, the Grand Lodge of Scotland was organized a few years later.

[15] Maynard Solomon, *Mozart: A Life,* New York: HarperCollins Publishers, 1995. pp. 321-335.

[16] Alfonso Scirocco, *Garibaldi, Citizen of the World: A Biography,* Princeton, NJ: Princeton University Press, 2007. pp. 33, 121, 381-82.

In general, Freemasonry has continued its commitment to individual freedom, democratic ideals, and human development through the course of the Twentieth Century. It is instructive that in most countries where authoritarianism has become rooted, the government in power has taken steps to destroy the institution. In Mussolini's Italy, Franco's Spain, Hitler's Germany, Hirohito's Japan, Lenin's Russia, Mao's China, Saddam's Iraq, Kim's North Korea, and in other places where liberty has been attacked, Freemasonry has been suppressed.[17] It has always risen like the mythical phoenix out of the ashes, however. Perhaps the most impressive modern example is the current revival of Freemasonry in Russia.

Freemasonry's core however, remains in the English-speaking part of the world, particularly England, and the United States. In the Twentieth Century, Masonic membership numbers experienced several ups and downs. Beginning in 1900, Freemasonry experienced steady growth in the United States, reaching approximately 2 million members in 1930. This was roughly 9% of the white, male, adult population of the nation at the time. Soon after, Masonic membership declined due to the stress of the Great Depression. In the post-war period, the Craft again experienced a boom as U.S. membership peaked at around 4.15 million members in the year 1959.[18]

In recent decades, Masonic membership has declined significantly. In 2020, there were approximately 900,000 Masons in the United States.[19] There are no complete statistics for world membership. Some have estimated that world-wide membership peaked at around 6 million

---

[17] Jasper Ridley, *The Freemasons: A History of the World's Most Powerful Secret Society,* New York: Arcade Publishing, 2001. pp. 236-56.
[18] Masonic Service Association of North America. "Membership Totals since 1924." MSA. Web, 2014. http://www.msana.com/msastats.asp
[19] Ibid.

members in 1960. An educated guess is that membership in 2020 was roughly about 1.5 million men around the world.

Enough about statistics. The important thing now to remember is that you are part of an organization that is hundreds of years old, with a proud history of expanding human knowledge, of defending freedom of thought and liberty of conscience. Be proud of your heritage! Almost anywhere in the world you will be able to find a "Brother." It is a truism that we notice what we look for. You will find that now that you are aware of the significance of the Square and Compasses, you will start to see these Masonic symbols everywhere. I remember that once I became a Freemason, I started to see rings, lapel pins, bumper stickers, and license plates everywhere I looked! For the first time in my life, I also began to take notice of Masonic lodge buildings. I'd passed by some of them for years and it never crossed my mind as to what they were.

The same thing will probably happen to you. Embrace this experience of Masonic recognition. If you see a man wearing a Masonic ring, shake hands with him. Ask him what lodge he attends. You will be surprised at the reaction you get. More often than not he will treat you as if you are friends, or as if you have some kind of shared connection. Want to know a real Masonic secret? *You do have a connection with this stranger.* He has gone through the same basic ceremonies and rites that you have experienced. He has taken the same oath and obligation that you swore to uphold. By the very fact of wearing that ring you know that he is of a mature disposition, is an upright, honest man, and that he believes in an ultimate Creator of the universe. To sum up, you know that he believes in the "Brotherhood of Man, under the Fatherhood of God." That's something to be cherished, if you ask me. Think about it: you never have to go through the world alone or friendless again. There will always be someone you can find who understands you and is sympathetic. In the future you will undoubtedly hear Brethren complain about the rising cost of membership. Dues keep going up every year, like everything else. What price would you put on this connection? What would you be willing to pay to acquire over a million brothers around the world? Think about it.[20]

---

[20] In a recent article, Daniel Akst explores the decline of friendship and the increasing atomization of American life. Until recently, having close friends was the norm for most men. They provided support, guidance, advice, and an emotional network that was considered a necessity for a healthy life. Akst explores the phenomenon of the busy—but empty existence in American society. See "America: Land of Loners," *The Wilson Quarterly*, Summer 2010, The Woodrow Wilson Center for Scholars, Washington, DC.

Masonic trivia:

Fourteen U.S. Presidents were Freemasons. They were, in order: George Washington, James Monroe, Andrew Jackson, James K. Polk, James Buchanan, Andrew Johnson, James A. Garfield, William McKinley, Theodore Roosevelt, William Howard Taft, Warren G. Harding, Franklin D. Roosevelt, Harry S. Truman, Lyndon B. Johnson, and Gerald R. Ford.

Andrew Jackson served as Grand Master of Tennessee. Harry S. Truman served as Grand Master of Missouri. James Buchanan, the only President from Pennsylvania, served as a District Deputy Grand Master for the Grand Lodge of Pennsylvania.

A Pennsylvania Lodge Room

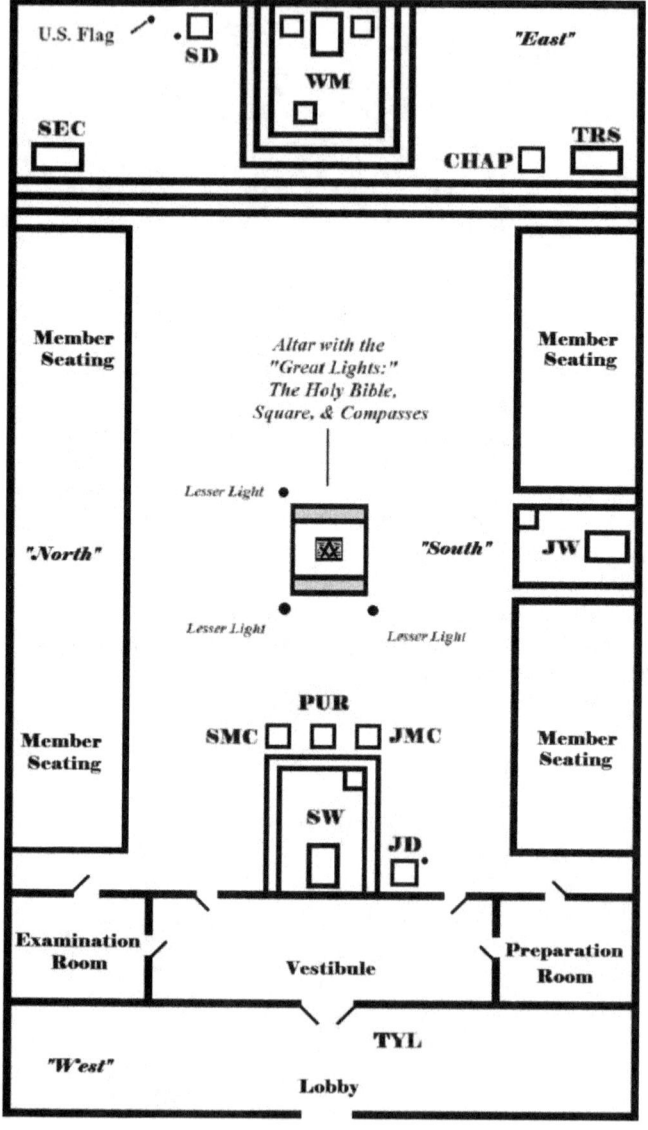

2. THE LODGE ROOM

As a Freemason, you will spend much of your time in the lodge room. It can be a confusing place. The first regular meeting I attended was a blur. Brethren were sitting all over the place, moving around, wearing various aprons or insignia and speaking a strange dialogue. I'd received some instruction about the lodge room and its officers during my degrees, but I'd forgotten most of it. I'm sure you are in a similar situation.

Don't worry. The purpose of this chapter is to look at the physical layout of the room, the places of the officers, their duties, and some of the symbolism of this important place. I can't guarantee that you will become an expert, but I can promise that you will be more comfortable at your next meeting. As we progress through the chapter, you will need to consult the diagram on the preceding page.

Remember that the lodge room is a representation of the Temple of Solomon at Jerusalem. There is an altar, three officers that supervise "the work," and furnishings used during degrees. Let's start with basics. The lodge room has four sides; East, West, North, and South. These have nothing to do with geography, however. Lodge buildings are not oriented in any particular direction. The north side of the lodge room seldom points to "true north." The **East** is where the Master presides over the meeting. Many other officers have their places there. During a meeting, the attention of the Brethren will usually be focused toward the East. The **West** end is the second most important side of the room. This is where a second group of officers sit. This is also where the entrance to the lodge room is. The **South** side is where one final officer sits. The **North** end contains no officers, just regular seating.

All lodges are laid out in the same manner. In a few older buildings, the design might be slightly different because they were "grandfathered" in. The exceptions to this design are very, very rare.

The **Lobby** is the last "public" space in the lodge. No one but Freemasons can proceed beyond this area. This is where Brethren sign in, put on their aprons, and generally socialize with each other before meetings start.

Entering the double doors (called the "Outer Door"), you are in the **Vestibule**. Most lodges don't use this area very much. It is a transitional area that prepares you for entering the actual lodge room itself. Two doors here lead to the lodge room proper. Before meetings, members can enter the lodge through either one. Once a meeting starts, however, only the right-hand (southern) door may be used.

Flanking the vestibule are two small, important rooms: the Preparation Room, and the Examination Room. The **Preparation Room** is used by candidates to get ready to receive their Masonic degrees. I'd recommend that you poke around the Preparation room some time. You probably don't remember much about it, I'm sure!

The **Examination Room** is used by visitors to the lodge. One of your privileges as a Master Mason is the right to visit other lodges in the Commonwealth. However, a visitor must be "vouched for" by a member of that lodge, or he must be "examined" in order to verify his credentials as a Freemason. Normally, a visitor must produce a "valid" dues card from his lodge, or proof of membership, and pass an examination given in this room. Don't let this discourage you from visiting. The examination is not difficult—for a Freemason!

Moving from the vestibule through the **Inner Doors**, we enter the **Lodge Room**. The first thing that naturally

catches one's eye is the **Holy Altar**. Symbolically, it represents the central place that the Creator should have in your life. Remember that a requirement of membership is the belief in a Supreme Being. Freemasons don't care what denomination, or religion, a man belongs to, just that he believes in a power greater than mankind. The Masonic term for this creator is "The Great Architect of the Universe," or the G.A.O.T.U.

Upon the Altar are the three "Great Lights" of Freemasonry: The Holy Bible, Square, and Compasses. In lodges with members from other religions, other sacred books can be found here. In Pennsylvania most lodges use the Holy Bible since the state is overwhelmingly Judeo-Christian in its composition. When a meeting is in progress, the Bible must be open, and when the Bible is closed, the meeting is over. Around the Altar are three "Lesser Lights." They represent the sun, the moon, and the Master of the lodge. When a lodge is meeting, they are lit. When the meeting is over, they are extinguished. More about these lights later. There is general seating for members on the North and South sides of the room. Now that you have an idea of the geography of the lodge, let's move on to the officers within it.

Officers of the Lodge

At the East end of the lodge is a raised platform which has three steps. On top of this platform is a dais upon which are three chairs, and a waist-high pedestal.

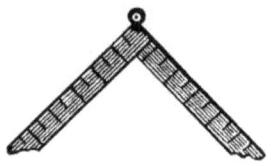

This is the station of the **Worshipful Master (WM)**. The Master is the president, if you will, of the lodge. He is elected for a one-year term and is responsible for everything concerning that lodge. He presides over meetings, he is on every committee, and he plans all major activities for that year. He is to be obeyed in all matters, although his power is not absolute. He does most of the speaking during regular meetings. Around his neck is his jewel of office: the square.

The Master is addressed as "worshipful" because it is an old English form of respect, similar to "honorable," or your honor." Beside the Master is a pedestal. On it are his gavel, a stone upon which he gavels meetings to order, a

copy of the Constitution of the Grand Lodge of
Pennsylvania, the lodge's individual by-laws, a Bible, and
some additional Masonic tools. At the foot of the pedestal,
in a frame, is the Warrant and Constitution of the lodge.
This is the paper issued by the Grand Master creating the
lodge, and authorizing it to meet. Many are very old, some
dating back to the 1800's or even earlier. The Warrant must
be displayed here during meetings for the lodge to legally
meet. If the building were to burn down, the first thing to be
saved should be the Warrant and Constitution.

The Master is the only member of the lodge who
stands throughout the meeting. The chairs behind him are
seldom used, except occasionally by visiting Masonic
dignitaries. You will also notice that the Master wears a
hat during the meeting—a formal top hat, along with a
tuxedo, complete with tails. Pennsylvania is a very formal
state. All officers in our lodges should wear tuxedos with
tails, and white gloves. All regular members should wear
suits, or at least coats and ties.

At the opposite end from the Master, in the West end
of the room, is the seat of the second-ranking member of the
lodge, the **Senior Warden (SW)**. The Senior Warden could
be termed the vice-president of the lodge. He is also elected
for a one-year term and is responsible for supporting and
assisting the Master. He presides over meetings if the Master

is absent. He is dressed similarly to the Worshipful Master except he wears no hat. Around his neck is his jewel of office: the level. Because election requirements are so strict in Pennsylvania, except in extremely rare instances, the Senior Warden is the heir apparent and will succeed the Master during the next Masonic year. He has a pedestal similar to the Master's with similar implements upon it.

One additional element to the Senior Warden's station is a miniature column that rests upon his pedestal. He uses it in opening and closing lodge ceremonies and to signal to the brethren when the meeting is open or closed.

On the South side of the lodge room is a small platform where the **Junior Warden (JW)** sits. He is the third ranking member of the lodge. He too serves a one-year term and is responsible for supporting and assisting the Senior Warden and the Master, in any way he can. He presides over meetings if the Senior Warden and Worshipful Master are absent. He is dressed similarly to the other two ranking officers. Around his neck is his jewel of office: the plumb. His pedestal is similar to the other two, and he also has a column which he uses to help open and close meetings. The Junior Warden plays a very important role in the degrees. He is the first Mason who spoke to you when you were in the preparing room asking to be made a Mason. He also announces the presence of the Candidate seeking entry into the lodge room. If the meeting recesses for a short time, he is charged with keeping order in the room. He will normally be elected Master in two years.

At the South East corner of the lodge room is the desk of the **Treasurer (TRS)**. He is the fourth ranking member of the lodge and is also annually elected by the membership. Around his neck is his jewel of office: the crossed keys. His duties are of course, financial. He is responsible for keeping the books and seeing that the finances of the lodge are in good order. He must be one of the officers that countersigns all checks for the payment of goods and services. The other signees are the Secretary and the Worshipful Master. He gives a report to the membership during every meeting detailing income, expenses, payments, and the overall cash balance of the lodge. Although technically anyone is eligible to run for this office, because of the work, responsibility, and trust involved, a long-time member of the lodge is usually elected. Often, he has been Worshipful Master. In many lodges, Treasurers serve for multiple terms. Since almost no lodge positions are paid, there is never very much competition for the duties and responsibilities of this position.

At the North East corner is the desk of the **Secretary (SEC)**, the fifth ranking officer of the lodge. He wears the crossed quills as his jewel of office. He is responsible for keeping the minutes of all stated and extra meetings. The Secretary helps compose, and mail, the monthly meeting notices. He is the point of contact for all correspondence from the Grand Lodge. All notices, changes of rules, and decisions or edicts from the Grand Lodge, come to his desk. He reads the minutes from the previous meetings, he coordinates degrees, he makes sure that membership cards are mailed out, that candidates are vetted—in short, the secretary does *all* the paperwork of the lodge. Like the Treasurer, in most lodges he is a Past Worshipful Master and is a repository of lodge wisdom and custom. He is the strong right arm and support of the Master. It is no exaggeration to say that the Secretary is probably the most important member of the lodge. Any Freemason will tell you, that, if you have to choose between the Master or the Secretary suddenly dropping dead, it is better if the Master goes! Like the other officers, his term is for one year, but usually lodges refuse to let a good secretary retire. Secretaries are sometimes paid a trivial salary. Most serve for many years. Get to know the Secretary of your lodge. You won't regret it.

The next two officers have similar duties. Looking toward the East, on the right hand of the Worshipful Master, is the **Senior Deacon (SD)**. Looking toward the West, on the right hand of the Senior Warden, is the **Junior Deacon (JD)**. Both officers wear a jewel representing a dove carrying a sprig of olive. Both Deacons carry messages and perform varied jobs during the stated meeting. The Senior Deacon carries messages for the Worshipful Master, usually to the Senior Warden. Since the national flag is right beside his chair, he carries it to the Altar during the Flag Ceremony. The Junior Deacon carries messages within the lodge for the Senior Warden, usually to the Junior Warden. As they perform their messenger duties, both men carry a seven-foot-long staff, or wand, in their right hands. The Senior Deacon also plays an important role during degree work by assisting the conferring officer in the East. The Junior Deacon also performs the additional duty of escorting visitors or dignitaries around the lodge room. Both officers are appointed by the Master. The Senior Deacon is however, normally slated to move up to Junior Warden the following year. The Junior Deacon normally will move up to the Senior Deacon's position.

Both of these officers have made a real commitment to "moving up the line" and someday having the opportunity to become the Worshipful Master. As you observe meetings, you will notice that as an officer moves up to more senior positions in the lodge, he plays a more and more important role in the ceremonies and rituals of Masonry.

In front of the station of the Senior Warden in the West, are three identical chairs occupied by three identically dressed officers—all with swords at their sides. The swords give an important clue to the roles of these three officers. All are sentinels of one sort or another, and are authorized to carry weapons in the performance of their duties within the body of the open lodge. The officer in the middle is called the **Pursuivant (PUR)**. Around his neck is his jewel of office: the crossed swords. His duty is to guard the Outer Door of the lodge room and monitor anyone attempting to enter, or exit. If anyone wishes to enter the lodge once a meeting starts, he must knock on the Outer Door located in the Lobby. The Pursuivant, upon hearing the knock, rises and informs the Worshipful Master that someone wishes to enter. He then rises from his place, leaves the room, and investigates the disturbance. If a visitor is authorized to enter by the Worshipful Master, the Pursuivant escorts him into the lodge room and announces his presence to the brethren. This office is filled through appointment by the Worshipful Master, usually for one year. As with all lodge officers, the Pursuivant should be dressed formally in a tuxedo with tails, white gloves, as well as his jewel of office, apron, and sword.

On either side of the Pursuivant are two more officers with similar roles: the **Senior Master of Ceremonies (SMC)** and the **Junior Master of Ceremonies (JMC)**. Their jewels of office are the crossed batons. The Senior Master of Ceremonies sits on the Northern side of the Pursuivant, to his left. His duty is to attend, and guard the door of the Examination Room. If any strangers arrive in the course of a stated meeting, they must be tested to determine if they are Masons. They are conducted into the Examination Room and, after being examined by an appointed committee, are allowed to enter the lodge room.

First, they must knock on the door separating the Examination Room from the lodge. The knock must be answered by the Senior Master of Ceremonies who determines who it is. After being given permission to enter by the Worshipful Master, they are escorted into the lodge. The Senior Master of Ceremonies has another important duty. At the start of every meeting, the Holy Bible must be opened as it lays upon the Altar. At the end of the meeting, it must be closed. It is the Senior Master of Ceremonies who performs these ritualistic tasks.

To the South of the Pursuivant, on his right side, sits the Junior Master of Ceremonies. His duties are very similar to the Senior Master of Ceremonies. His main concern is the door to the Preparation Room. During degrees, every time a candidate wishes to enter the lodge room, he must knock on the door that separates the Preparation Room from the body of the open lodge. This knock must be answered by the Junior Master of Ceremonies. He determines who has knocked, informs the Worshipful Master, and then allows the candidate to enter. A known member wishing to enter the lodge can also be escorted by the Junior Master of Ceremonies through the Vestibule door. This is after the Pursuivant has identified him, and if the Worshipful Master consents to his entry.

The doors to the lodge room are considered sacred during meetings. They are so important that the Pursuivant and the two Masters of Ceremonies are the only brethren permitted to even *touch* them!

Both of these positions are filled by the Worshipful Master for one year. Many Brethren serve in them in order to get more familiar with lodge ritual, but they are in no sense a commitment to a future position in the lodge like the office of Deacon might be. Often a brother will take this office for a year, and then return to the "sidelines" the next year.

There is one more officer left within the lodge room, and he plays another small, but vital, role in all Masonic gatherings. His chair is right beside the Treasurer's desk.

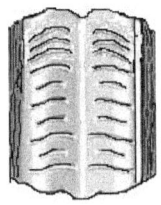

He is the **Chaplain (CHAP)**. He wears a small open book as his jewel of office. It normally represents the Holy Bible, but remember that *any* sacred text can be used within the lodge, depending on one's religion. Christianity and Freemasonry are *not* synonymous, although in our state most lodges are generally made up of Christian members.

The Chaplain's duties are to lead the lodge in prayer during the opening and closing ceremonies. He also recites a prayer during the First Degree when a Candidate is made a Freemason. Prayers are also usually a part of any additional lodge ceremony not connected with regular meetings. Finally, when a Brother's family requests a Masonic funeral, the Chaplain leads the lodge in paying a last tribute to the deceased. Prayers during Masonic gatherings are generally addressed to "The Great Architect of the Universe."

The Chaplain is an appointed office for one year. In lodges with members who happen to be clergymen, it is often the case that they are usually asked to fill this chair. Any member of the lodge, however, is eligible.

We now come to the loneliest of all the officers that serve the lodge: the **Tyler (TYL)**. His jewel of office, hanging around his neck, is the sword. He also carries a real one, like the Masters of Ceremonies and the Pursuivant. He guards the outer door that separates the Lobby from the Vestibule. He is also in charge of greeting visitors to the

lodge before meetings, and making sure that they sign in. He determines if they can be vouched for, or if they need an examination. He is also in charge of making sure that the aprons of the lodge are available in the lobby for the use of lodge members. During the meetings of the lodge, the Tyler stays outside and secures the entrance, making sure that no unauthorized persons come near. An informal role of most Tylers is to make sure that the dining area is ready for use after the meeting. If any food is cooking, he also makes sure to give it a stir so that nothing burns!

After each Masonic meeting comes the fellowship hour where refreshments and food are served in the lodge's dining room. In my opinion, this period is just as important as the actual meeting itself. This is a time for brethren to relax, get something to eat, gossip, and talk about the meeting, and the lodge in an informal way. This is an important time when the bonds of brotherly love and affection are strengthened.

Finally, there is one last officer that I need to cover. He is as important as anyone in the lodge. He has no jewel of office, however. He has no special place to sit, and he is appointed for one night only. And yet, in many ways his influence upon Masonry is profound. He is the first person that a Candidate meets on his first night at the lodge.

He is the **Guide**. His role is to meet the Candidate, conduct him into the preparing room, and get him ready to receive his degrees in Freemasonry. During the ceremony, he is responsible for leading the Candidate around the body of the open lodge, prompting him if needed, and smoothing the way for the new member to take his oath and obligation.

Guides should be knowledgeable about the ceremonies of Freemasonry. They should explain, as far as possible, what is happening, and what is to come. In a real sense, the Guide is a Candidate's introduction to the entire world of Masonry. A bad, ill-educated Guide, can ruin a new member before he even becomes a Mason. Only experienced, kindly, Masonically well-educated brethren should be entrusted with this important job.

In past generations, there was a lot of foolishness associated with degree nights. The rites being secret, no one really knew what to expect when they asked to become a Mason. Unfortunately, for some reason, teasing and joking became the norm. Candidates would be asked if they were ready to endure pain, humiliation, or if they were ready to "ride the goat" around the lodge. Hints, winks, and laughter at the Candidate's expense were popular. Thank goodness those days are mostly over! Degrees are supposed to be solemn, dignified, and serious. Even though few men believe the myths about Masonic rites, most Candidates are very nervous when they first join. This is where the Guide plays his most important role. If he can give the new Mason a positive experience, it will go a long way toward strengthening that new Brothers' life-long commitment to the Craft.

Finally, every lodge has three annually elected **Trustees**. They are charged with overseeing the business and financial health of the lodge. They are usually brethren who have served as Worshipful Master in the past and wish to continue to serve the organization. They vaguely resemble a board of directors. The Secretary, Treasurer, and Worshipful Master do not answer to them and they do not instruct those officers. They can best be understood as a legal protection for the lodge organization, and as an additional source of oversight and institutional wisdom.

Masonic products

A big question: What should I buy? There are rings, watches, charms, tie clips, pins, hats, aprons, shirts, belts, DVD's, plaques, pictures, ties, sun visors, knives, wallets, and thousands of other items for sale. You can go broke buying Masonic products. Really, you can.

So, what you should do? As always, my advice is to go slow. There is no hurry. People have been making Masonic merchandise for hundreds of years. Whatever you see, this will *not* be the only one made, and it won't be the *only* chance you will ever have to buy it.

Hopefully, your lodge will have presented you with a lapel pin and a Bible. That's a good start. A good Masonic ring is probably something you will want and need. That ring will attract a lot of attention by other brethren. I can't even count the men I've met who have noticed the ring and struck up a conversation because of my ring. So go ahead and get one. Look to your pocketbook and to your personal style when buying a ring. A short search of the internet reveals lots of companies selling rings. They range in price from around $25 for a fake gold ring, to thousands for diamond encrusted masterpieces. Many small firms offer stainless steel, or sterling silver rings for $100 or so.

Get something conservative, something that won't go out of style. A plain ring with a blue or black stone or background, with the Square and Compasses on it should serve you well. You wear it on the ring finger of your right hand, with the compass points toward you—Pennsylvania style.

The author's ring.

So now what? You've gone through your degrees and become a Master Mason. You've received a monthly notice and you're looking forward to your first meeting as a full-fledged Mason. What can you expect? What is life like as a Freemason in a lodge?

First, *be prepared for some sort of letdown.* Think back. Up until now, you've been the center of attention. Your sponsor had you fill out a petition. A committee visited your home and interviewed you and your family. When you went to the lodge for your degrees, it seemed like everyone wanted to shake your hand and talk to you. It felt like you were the most important man in the lodge. You were. That's the operative word here: *were.* Now, however, you're just another member—and the newest one at that.

On the night of *my* first regular meeting, I arrived excited. I wore my best suit. Members straggled in. There didn't seem to be many of them—not like on my degree nights. I filled out a members slip, tied on my apron, and walked into the lodge room.

It was interesting, confusing, and somewhat boring. The ceremony of opening the lodge was eye-catching and solemn. It was hard to follow though, what with the various officers moving around the room, but it held my attention. Then came what could only be described as a typical business meeting. Visitors were recognized. Minutes of the last meeting were read and approved. Minutes from an extra meeting were read and approved. Letters, notices, and circulars were read. Petitions for membership were read. Committees were named. Reports by committees already in existence were given and approved. Trustees spoke. Building association members spoke. The Treasurer made *his* report and it was approved. I started to get a little fidgety. Finally, the meeting closed with ceremony and a prayer. Walking out, I smelled coffee in the dining room. Although the meeting had started at 7:30 and it was only 9, I felt like it had lasted a lot longer. I was so punch drunk that I broke my no coffee rule in the evening. The food was just doughnuts. After a few minutes of small talk, I left.

On the drive home I asked myself: "Is this *it*? Is this all they do? They have 16 meetings a year. Are they all like this? Have I made a mistake in joining?"

Don't be surprised if you find yourself feeling this way. What should you do? Here's a second thing to remember: *don't panic.* Don't give in to the bad feelings. Don't get discouraged. Remember that 90% of life is just showing up! Go to meetings. Let me repeat: go to as many lodge meetings as you can. You can't get anything valuable from Masonry if you don't participate in it. Remember, that from now on, it is up to *you* to actively seek meaning within the Fraternity. You are no longer the passive Candidate, receiving enlightenment. You have some work to do.

The year I joined, I attended all monthly stated meetings, all extra meetings, and the monthly school of instruction held by our district. It added up to 30 meetings that first year. I'm not suggesting that you must do what I did, but my point is that you have to make an *effort* to learn. You've just spent several months, and a considerable sum of money, in order to become a Freemason. How about an additional investment of patience and concentration? Masonry is a gradual process. You don't get Enlightenment all at once. Try to hold on to that thought.

Third: *remember that Freemasonry is an eighteenth-century institution.* The manners, the language, the procedures, in short, everything about it, are from the 1700's. In this day and age, people just don't talk the way they do during Masonic meetings. They don't have the same mannerisms. In many ways, attending a meeting is like traveling back in time. It would be astounding if you *weren't* confused at first! Give yourself (and Masonry) some time. What's your hurry? There is no prize for being the first Brother to totally understand the Craft and all its inner workings and philosophy. This is a lifetime project. Again, let me repeat: take your time.

The Eighteenth century was the age of classicism, an age that revered the classic mode of thinking. It looked to the ancient Greeks and Romans for inspiration.[21] One way of looking at reality is to divide human understanding into two distinct modes: classical and romantic. Classical thinking perceives the world as consisting of underlying forms. Romantic thinking is concerned with appearance and surface realities.

The romantic mode is thought to be inspirational, imaginative, creative, and emotional. Feelings predominate one's perspective, rather than facts and rules. Art is part of the realm of romantic thought—at least it often is. The appearance of things is what is important, not their underlying form.

The classic perspective proceeds by reason, laws, and is concerned with understanding the underlying forms of reality itself. In western culture, law, medicine, and science are within the classic modes of understanding. Traditionally, they have

---

[21] The following is loosely adapted from Robert M. Pirsig's *Zen and the Art of Motorcycle Maintenance: An Inquiry into Values,* New York: Bantam Books, 1976. pp. 66-9.

been perceived as masculine, while romantic modes are assigned a feminine label.

In the last century, the conflict between classic and romantic understanding has become somewhat destructive. They seem to be mutually hostile. Popular culture seems to be mainly romantic, concerned with style and surface. For many men, work and its demands, are part of the world of classic understanding. Too many of us feel like we have to live mutually exclusive lives. Some Brethren I've talked to complain that Masonic meetings remind them of their jobs. If they want dull, boring, formal, empty interaction, they can just stay at work. Why should they come to a meeting for more of the same?

This is a fair criticism. My answer would be though, you're only looking at a part of the Masonic program. Freemasonry is an attempt to *combine* the classic and the romantic modes and invent an entirely new way of understanding human life. The meeting is formal, without question. There is a lot of ceremony, no doubt about it. This is the ugly, boring, awkward side of the classical. But combined with this formality is a rich use of symbol, myth, stories, costumes, and visual aids. This is where Masonry attempts to appeal to the romantic side of human nature. Freemasonry is designed to reach *both* our romantic, and intellectual natures. I'm not sure if this was the original plan, but this is how it has developed. The goal is to entertain, to teach, to uplift—in a word—to *Enlighten* its membership.

It's an ambitious agenda. Few in western history have attempted such a goal. Don't expect things to be easy. Freemasonry teaches that you have four basic obligations in life: to God, your family, your profession, and finally, to Masonry. *Keep this order in mind.* Don't neglect your responsibilities. Keep them in balance. I've known men who spent virtually 6 nights out of every 7 going to

Masonic gatherings. In the literature of Freemasonry there are many references to "Masonic Widows." Don't contribute to this phenomenon.

The beehive. Symbol of industry and teamwork.

But the questions remain: "What do I do now? How do I get involved? What Direction should I follow? How busy should I get?" There are no easy answers. Every lodge is different. Every Brother is different. We all have individual interests or talents. We all have different needs. What worked for me was first, *an attitude of humbleness.* I asked myself: "what does this new organization that I have joined—this Lodge—need? What can I give to it? What can I contribute, not for any personal reason…not because I'm going to get anything out of it. What can I give, just to give?"

That was the way I started. I was asked by the Senior Warden if I would oblige him and fill a minor officer's chair the following year: Senior Master of Ceremonies. I agreed but warned him that I didn't know a lot of the ritual, and didn't really understand much about meetings yet. He said that was ok, and told me there would be no undue demands placed on me.

It was a beginning. I went to every meeting, listened, and learned. At the end of every year, I was asked to fill a slightly higher position. With each year, my commitment to the lodge grew. My fellow members got to know and trust me. They could see evidence of my desire to help. At every step, I kept asking: "Am I doing this so that I can get recognition and prestige, or am I doing this to help the lodge?" I can honestly say that had there been others willing to step ahead of me, I would have gladly remained a humble member. After six years, I was elected Worshipful Master of the lodge. I felt I had a good year, but I'm sure others could have done better. I ensured that other Brethren were ready to take over in the future, so in that sense I think I was a success as Worshipful Master.

I didn't plan this journey "through the chairs." It just happened. Gradually, I found other ways to help, and I found other members asking themselves how *they* could get involved. We helped each other. One humorous example involved the lodge building itself. Our lodge had been built in the 1960's. The interior had been neglected and ignored. The lodge was pretty bare of any decoration. A few pictures were hung randomly. The walls were cheap, dark brown, imitation wood paneling. The Vestibule was crowded with old furniture. The Preparation and Examination Rooms were used as storage spaces. The Lobby was cut in half by a huge wood and glass display counter that was used to store Masonic products for sale. It prevented anyone from mingling and talking before meetings. The whole building was dark, cramped, and felt neglected.

One night after a building committee meeting, I was talking with a few members about how the lodge looked to us. We all agreed that it was dark, depressing, and meanly furnished. It wasn't the kind of place that made you *want* to attend meetings. One brother looked at the display case and said: "I'd like to get rid of that monstrosity!" We decided we didn't have the authority to get rid of it, but one of us asked: "why don't we just push it out of the way against that wall?" We looked at each other, and then started to push. When we were done, all of us looked around uneasily. I think we were secretly expecting some of the older members to appear in righteous fury and yell at us for touching anything. But nothing happened. There was no earthquake. And then we saw that the entire lobby had suddenly changed. There was space! There was room to mingle, to breathe! The whole geography of the place was transformed. We went home happy.

At the next meeting, no one said anything about the change. We realized that the sky wasn't going to fall. From that small beginning grew a lodge decoration project. In the following years walls were painted, pictures put up, furniture moved, rooms cleaned out, and eventually our lodge became a showplace. The moral of the story is, I guess: *look for other like-minded men who truly want to contribute.* They're probably right there in front of you. Just open your eyes. And if you find them, don't neglect to try to learn something. You aren't the only one with ideas. Maybe someone else has a better way. Freemasonry isn't your own private preserve. It isn't a hobby either. It's more like a way of life. Don't expect to change everything just to suit yourself. Also, don't expect revolutionary changes. Just because you personally think something needs to be fixed, don't assume that everyone thinks that way. *Don't assume you know everything!*

Lodges are living organisms made up of imperfect men. Like the proverbial snowflake, no two are alike. The only difference between Masonic lodges and other organizations is that lodges are made of up members who are sworn to try to do right, to improve themselves, and to help others. Go slow and look around. Is there anything you can do to make your lodge better? How is the food after meetings? Are you a good cook? Could you help there? What about the committees for visiting the sick? Are they full? Does your lodge have a community outreach? A fundraiser? A special charity that it contributes to? Does it need new candidate's clothing or tuxedos for officers? How about new paraphernalia? Does the grass need to be cut? Is attendance a problem? Do you have ideas? Once again, look around and see where you can contribute.

One last word. Some lodges are in trouble. Some seem to be controlled by a small group of men who don't want change, or any new ideas. They don't want to let anyone into their group. They tend to hold on to most of the administrative and financial positions and will *not* loosen their grip. Nothing moves in these lodges without their say-so. Attendance is low, meetings are boring and depressing. There is no spirit of brotherly love and affection. If this describes your lodge what can be done?

My advice is to try the methods I've already outlined. Maybe things aren't so bad. Maybe there are other members that you can work with. Give it some time. Try hard. After a while—and everyone has a limit to the amount of patience they have—you might have to consider giving up. In that case, my advice is to start looking for another lodge. You can transfer your membership in Pennsylvania. You aren't tied to a lodge for life. Don't give up your membership in Masonry, just find another place to practice it. It's a big step, but one you should consider should you get to the end of your rope.

A LODGE MEETING

Perhaps it might be useful to explore what happens at a typical meeting. If nothing else, this might help you understand what is going on and the purpose for each action taken during the gathering. Much of your formal time as a Freemason will be spent in lodge participating in such meetings. First, the formal name for a meeting is "The Monthly Stated Meeting." You will know the date and time because it will be *stated* in your monthly notice that you receive from your lodge Secretary. Traditionally, notices are sent by mail, although recently the Right Worshipful Grand Master has begun to encourage lodges to send them *via* email. Printing and mailing costs add up and could be used in other, better ways. Notices must be sent so that they are received by members well ahead of meetings—usually a week.

Notices have a common form in Pennsylvania. Usually, they contain four pages. On the front is the name and number of the lodge and its founding date. On the back are listed the officers and committees of the lodge, along with a list of living Past Masters. On page two is the program of that month's meeting, or meetings. If Degrees are being conferred, an "Extra Stated Meeting" will be held and that date will be included. The full names and addresses of anyone petitioning to join the lodge will also be in the notice. This is a requirement from the Grand Lodge. Finally, any special announcements or messages are included. A progress report for the year will list membership numbers, deaths, and any other losses up to the present date.

Meetings are standardized. The agenda normally consists of the opening ceremony, greeting of visitors, reading of minutes, communications, announcements, the program for the evening, reports of committees, reading and payment of any bills with the Treasurer's report, and the closing ceremony.

At 7:30 PM, the Worshipful Master calls the lodge to order, and directs the Pursuivant to "Tyle" the lodge. Tyle means to close all doors and make sure that they are guarded so that intruders cannot approach. The lodge is now cut off from the outside—*profane*—world. Then the opening ceremony is conducted. The Holy Bible is opened on the Altar by the Senior Master of Ceremonies. After the Flag ceremony with the Pledge of Allegiance, visitors to the lodge are greeted and welcomed. Next, the minutes of the previous meeting (or meetings) are read by the Secretary and approved. Letters, announcements, or any other communications to the lodge are also read at this time. Finally, any petitions for membership are announced. A committee is appointed to investigate petitioners, and report back to the lodge. If investigations have been completed, the potential member is voted on by the Brethren. A ballot box is placed upon the Altar and a vote taken. Most lodges should have a program for the evening: a special event, speaker, or a presentation of some sort. It is at this point it should take place. Next, any reports of the standing committees are given and any problems, or actions needed, are discussed. Finally, bills are read, the Treasurer gives a report on the financial health of the lodge, and the closing ceremony is performed. The Bible is then closed.

On one level, it *is* simply a meeting like any other. It can be boring. It is somewhat like paying bills, or checking a bank statement. Not compelling, but necessary. What can't be expressed on paper is the stateliness, the dignity, the magic, if you will, of the meeting. Masonic gatherings are filled with stylized behavior. The language used by the officers, the mannerisms of the Brethren when they address the Master, the voting procedures—all are done according to a severe ritualistic code. With concentration, understanding, and an open frame of mind, one can briefly attain an almost higher state of being for the evening.

If you have never participated in a meeting, or run a committee, or spoken before groups, Freemasonry is a chance to test yourself and learn. Too often we seem to be mere cogs in a large, impersonal system. It sometimes doesn't matter if one contributes or not. In Freemasonry, the individual truly *is* important. He really *can* make a contribution. If you decide to "go through the chairs" and work your way up to Worshipful Master, the opportunities for leadership experience are great. The year I was Worshipful Master, I was the head of a lodge with assets of several hundred thousand dollars, an annual budget of over $50,000, and 350 members. For an entire year, I was involved in every aspect of the organization. The best part about the experience was that, due to the requirements for election, I knew that I had *earned* my way to the top. How many organizations really promote solely on merit? The lodge is one of the few that I know of.

As I've said elsewhere, give the meetings a chance. Don't tune out. *Keep coming* to them! Nothing good comes without effort. Be patient and be persevering!

Definitions you will find useful

Bondman: person who is not free, who is subject to another.
Bourne: a boundary line, a limit of some sort; a border.
Clandestine: hidden, usually for some illegal, or illicit reason.
Dispensation: permission to do something out of the ordinary.
Dispatch: to do something quickly, promptly, and with speed.
Equivocation: to be evasive, to use ambiguous language.
Eunuch: a male who has been castrated.
Gauge: a measuring stick or rod.
Globes: earth and sky; symbolizes Masonry's universality.
Golden Fleece: the highest order of Hapsburg knighthood.
Hele: from old Anglo-Saxon, meaning to hide, or conceal.
Libertine: one who acts with no moral restraint whatsoever.
Meridian: the highest point of anything, the zenith.
Mote: Anglo-Saxon word meaning "may."
Oblong: having the shape of a rectangle, length greater than width.
Oriental: having to do with the east. From the Latin *oriens*.
Parian: a type of marble found in the Greek islands.
Penal: of, or having to do with punishment.
Shade: an area or space of partial darkness or obscurity.
Star and Garter: one of the highest orders of English knighthood.
Tarry: to wait, or to delay.
Work: it can mean Masonic degree conferrals, or business.
Wretch: outcast; a despicable being; utterly without merit.

Entered Apprentice's Song[22]
by Mathew Birkhead, 1722

Come, let us prepare,
We Brothers that are
Assembled on merry occasion;
Let's drink, laugh and sing,
Our Wine has a Spring,
Here's health to an Accepted Mason!
Mason!

The World is in pain,
Our secrets to gain,
And still let them wonder and gaze on;
station,
They ne'er can divine
The word or the sign,
Of a Free and an Accepted Mason!

'Tis this, and 'tis that,
They cannot say what,
Why so many Great Men of the Nation
face on;
Should aprons put on,
To make themselves one
With a Free and an Accepted Mason!

Great Kings, Dukes and Lords,
Have laid by their swords,
Our Mystr'y to put a good Grace
And ne'er been ashamed
To hear themselves named
With a Free and an Accepted

Antiquity's pride
We have on our side,
And it maketh men just in their

There's naught but what's good,
To be understood
By a Free and an Accepted Mason!

Then join Hand in Hand,
To each other Stand;
Let's be merry, and put a bright

What mortal can boast
So Noble a Toast
As a Free and an Accepted Mason!

I really like this poem. I read it years ago somewhere and it perfectly captures for me the mood, the feeling of *Brotherhood* that a lodge should have. It was written to be sung during dinner after the meeting. Lodges don't sing much nowadays, but hopefully your lodge has this kind of *spirit*!

---

[22] Web.http://www.masonic-poetry.org/poems/entapsng.htm Date: 22/06/2006

Freemasons were not always held in high esteem. Detail from an engraving entitled "Night," by William Hogarth. A drunken Worshipful Master (head of his lodge) is being conducted home by another Mason. They are identified by their aprons. The Master still wears his insignia of office. Drawing dates from 1738,

PART II

TAKE A SECOND STEP FORWARD:

MASONIC RITUAL

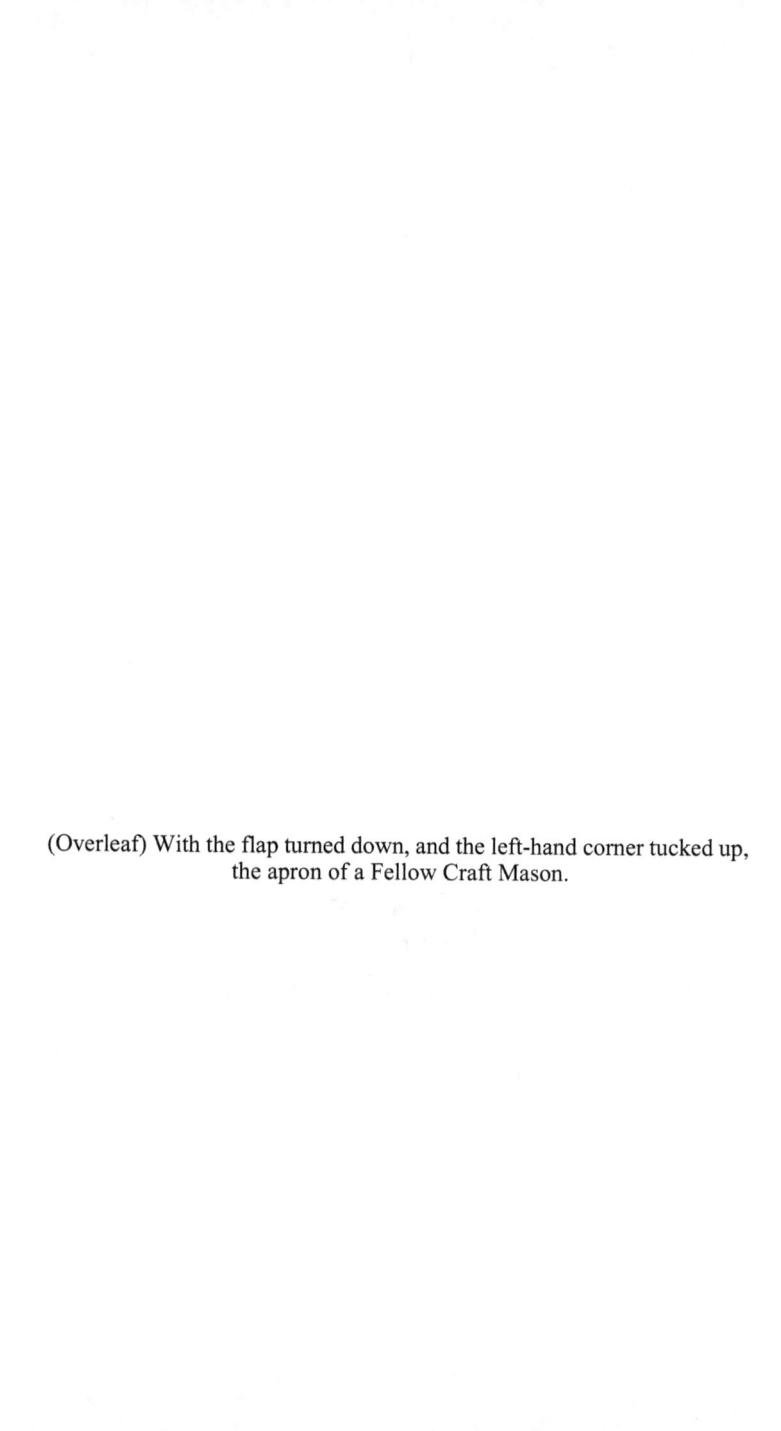

(Overleaf) With the flap turned down, and the left-hand corner tucked up, the apron of a Fellow Craft Mason.

4. THE FIRST DEGREE

Although I can't recall specifics, I've never forgotten the feelings I had the night I became a Freemason. I'd read very little about the Craft before deciding to join. My grandfather had been a member, and we kept his old Shriners' fez and a Scottish Rite ring with the family keepsakes. I remember looking at them as a child and wondering about their significance. All I knew was that George Washington had been a Freemason, and that some of my friends and acquaintances were enthusiastic about the organization. I figured the only way to find out was to join. There had to be something worthwhile there. I had the money, the curiosity, and the spare time, so why not try it?

After contacting a friend and going through the prerequisites, I was ready. On a Wednesday evening, September 20, 1995, I walked into the lodge with a check for $255 in my pocket for fees and dues. I remember some of my emotions from that night: nervous anticipation, puzzlement, awkwardness, pride, and some embarrassment.[23] That night, in a way I still can't explain, Freemasonry cast its spell on me. I'm still trying to figure out how. Many Freemasons say the same thing. It will probably take you most of your life to truly understand the degrees. What follows in this, and the next few chapters, is a recapitulation of the degrees, with a special emphasis on the mechanics of each one. I have written it to serve as a "cheat sheet" about the meaning of the Masonic degrees in our state, and the methods used in teaching morality with symbolism.

---

[23] For a good exploration of the feelings and emotions felt during the ceremony, I recommend Leo Tolstoy's *War and Peace*, Signet Classics, The New American Library, New York: 1968, pp. 426-41. In writing about Pierre Bezukhov's initiation, Tolstoy captures perfectly the awkwardness, the fear, and the awe that a candidate feels when taking this first Masonic step.

Pennsylvania Ritual

The Masonic degrees in Pennsylvania are different than those of other jurisdictions and Grand Lodges. The ritual is not dramatized. There is no music. No costumes are worn. There is not a large cast of players during the ceremonies. They consist largely of lectures and verbal instruction. The symbolism of each degree is explained, but very little is actually demonstrated. One might say that the action within the ritual is reinforced and defined by the words of the conferring officer. The candidate is required to use his imagination and supply his own meaning.

To give you an idea of how different Pennsylvania is from other states, consider the issue of time. In many states, an Entered Apprentice degree takes over two hours to complete. In Pennsylvania, one hour is usually sufficient. In some places, a Fellow Craft degree can last up to 90 minutes. In our Commonwealth, 45 minutes is a good average time. A Master Mason degree usually lasts 2 hours in our state. I have no idea how long a Third Degree lasts in other parts of the country. After attending about a dozen in three different jurisdictions, I've never witnessed the end of one! Starting at 7 p.m., the degrees I've attended were still going strong when I left at 11 p.m. In Pennsylvania, one extra brother is needed for a degree in order to guide the candidate. The conferring officer does most of the speaking. By contrast, in other states, nearly two dozen brethren are needed to fill various roles during a Third Degree.

The ritualistic language used in Pennsylvania is somewhat old-fashioned, but is direct, and to the point. While reminiscent of the 1700's, the vocabulary has only a few unfamiliar words, and they do not obscure the meaning of the ceremony for the candidate. In my humble opinion, no ritual can compare with ours for dignity, clarity, and stateliness.

A Masonic degree consists of six parts: the Preparation, the Circumambulation, the Obligation, the Recapitulation, the Investiture, and the Charge. We will take each of the degrees in turn and explore their structure and the symbolism contained within them.

One note here about secrecy. While Freemasonry is a private organization, it is wrong to consider it a secret society, with all aspects of it to be forever concealed from outsiders. Our buildings are clearly marked by signs. Membership lists can be obtained through Grand Lodge records. Most of our facilities are available for rent to the general public. Many lodges actually have "open houses" where tours are given to anyone who wishes to learn more about Freemasonry. The only things truly secret concerning our Pennsylvania ritual are the *specific* language used within it, the passwords, the grips and the special signs associated with each Degree. These are sacrosanct, but everything else can be revealed to the general public. Most of the ritual can be found on the internet or in a good public library. The real secrets of Freemasonry are within each Brother's soul. Let's begin with the First Degree—the Entered Apprentice Mason's Degree.

The Preparation. The degree process begins when the candidate enters the lodge building and is taken in hand by his Guide. After a few preliminaries in the lobby, he is taken to the Preparation Room to get ready, physically and spiritually, for his entrance into the Masonic brotherhood.

Under the direction of his Guide, the Candidate removes most of his clothing and dons a special blue garment that resembles a set of pajamas. He abandons all his money and takes off any valuable items that he normally wears. He also removes any metal objects from his person. He is barefoot and puts a slipper on his right foot. His pant leg is rolled up so that his left knee is bare. A rope—or "cable tow"—is knotted and wound once around his neck. Finally, he dons a blindfold—in Masonic terms, a "hoodwink." He is thus blind, helpless, defenseless, penniless, and isn't even wearing his own clothes.

The reason a Candidate is prepared this way is to teach him about certain aspects of the Brotherhood. You can't buy your way into Masonry, no matter how much money you have. The lodge is a place of peace, so any metal objects which could be used as weapons must be put aside. He wears a special outfit so that he is, in a sense, anonymous and without the advantages of wealth, fame, or social position. The purpose of the cable tow is to reinforce his helplessness in the face of the unknown. It is held by the Guide and is used to control his actions while in the lodge room. The blindfold is to teach him that he is spiritually blind, that he is seeking "Masonic Light," or wisdom.

Once he is ready, the Candidate waits in the Preparation Room with his Guide, listening to the muffled sounds of a meeting getting underway. Silence usually reigns in this little room as the Candidate contemplates what might happen next. When the proper time arrives, his hand is guided to a door knocker which he uses to knock three times in order to gain admission. His Guide speaks for him and tells whoever asks that a poor, blind, candidate for Freemasonry begs to be admitted and introduced into its mysteries. After his Guide gives the password, the

Candidate is then led into the darkened lodge room, told to kneel, and then is asked two questions. First, he is asked if he wants to join Freemasonry for economic advantage, or for any improper purpose. Then he is asked if he will affirm his faith in a Supreme Being. If he answers those questions correctly, he proceeds to the next stage of the Degree.

The Circumambulation. This is just an arcane term for circling someone, or something. In this stage of the Degree, the Candidate—still blind folded—is led by his Guide around the body of the open lodge three times. He does not know where he is going and must trust his Guide. He is actually circling the Altar with the officers of the lodge grouped around it. During each circuit he is stopped by each of the three senior-most lodge officers and asked why he has come here, and what is his business? His Guide replies that he has come to seek "Masonic Light" and wisdom. After giving the password, they proceed on. No lodge room is very big, yet I have known Brethren who swear they walked hundreds of yards during this part of the ceremony. It actually seems that way. Finally, the Candidate is told to stop. He is made to face the East, and take one step forward—the step of an Entered Apprentice Mason. Then he is told to kneel and his hands are placed around something. Since he is still hoodwinked, his actions are narrated for him. He is kneeling at the Altar. The object that he places his hands around, is a book—The Holy Bible, with the Square and Compasses upon it. He is told that the Oath he is about to take is old and is used for tradition's sake. Nothing in it is harmful, or against the laws of his country, state, or religion. The penalties mentioned in the Oath are symbolic only and are not to be taken literally.

The Obligation. This word is derived from the Latin *obligare*, "to bind."[24] Specifically, it is called the Oath and

---

[24] Roberts, p. 26.

Obligation since it consists of particular undertakings (obligations), as well as penalties (the oath), if one breaks one's word. The obligation part deals with secrecy of all kinds. One is to keep much of what one does and experiences as a Freemason secret and inviolate from the outside, "profane" world.[25] The obvious question that might occur at this point concerns the entire nature of the book you are now reading. What about the author's Masonic Oath and Obligation? Does everything I've written break my solemn vows? Well, this is not a simple question. Like many things in life, the answer is: "it depends."

In some jurisdictions around the nation all writing, or communications of *any* kind dealing with *any* Masonic information are considered a violation of one's oath. Many jurisdictions even forbid discussing Masonic matters on internet sites under penalty of expulsion from the Brotherhood! No public statements are permitted without the permission of the proper Masonic authorities. Some states seem to spend more energy throwing Brethren out of the Fraternity than in recruiting new members. Such rigid discipline seems to me to be detrimental to Masonry's roots as an organization that always encouraged freedom of thought, and spiritual development.

As I stated earlier, the Grand Lodge of Pennsylvania has a different philosophy. In Pennsylvania there are actually very few specific elements of Freemasonry that are absolutely secret and inviolate. The actual ritual language itself may not be written down or communicated to a nonmember. The specific articles of the oaths and obligations may not be discussed. The penalties may not be talked about. Finally, there are special handshakes, grips, signs, and passwords associated with each degree

---

[25] This term simply refers to those outside the Fraternity. It is an example of a general term in the English language used in a specific, purely Masonic way. There are many such examples of this phenomenon in Masonry.

which really *are* very private and must be kept secret. Everything else may be discussed with your friends and family.

In recent years, the Grand Master of Pennsylvania has even authorized the ritual of the three degrees to be printed, and copies given to each lodge. They are to be guarded carefully, of course. The reason this was done was because in any culture where information is handed down verbally from generation to generation, mistakes can creep into the language. To keep our ceremonies standard, the Grand Master decided that a written guide was required so that it could be consulted as needed by conferring officers. It is not to be used during conferral of degrees.

To continue. The Entered Apprentice is sworn to secrecy and promises to use discretion when talking about Masonic matters. He swears his oath and binds himself with traditional, horrible penalties, calling down vengeance from heaven if he should break his word. He agrees that if he breaks his promise he deserves to be killed, mutilated horribly, and buried in unconsecrated ground. Remember, that before the oath was administered, he was told that these penalties are not to be taken literally. They are traditional and are meant to impress upon everyone the solemnity of the promises just made. After this part of the ceremony, the Candidate swears "so help me God," and kisses the Holy Bible to additionally seal his promise.[26]

Then comes the most memorable part of the initiation ceremony. After once more praying to be brought to "Masonic Light," the Candidate's blindfold is suddenly

---

[26] I've always found it interesting that George Washington, on taking the Oath of office on April 30, 1789 incorporated this gesture into the ceremony. Harry Truman, upon taking the oath for the first time in 1945, also kissed the Holy Bible. Both men had served as Worshipful Masters. James Thomas Flexner, *George Washington and the New Nation (1783-1793)*, New York: Little, Brown and Company, 1969. p. 187. Also, see David McCullough, *Truman*, New York: Simon & Schuster, 1992. p. 347.

removed, and the lights are turned on in the lodge room. He kneels there, blinking, blinded, and confused. Gradually his sight is restored and he is able to make out the Altar, the Holy Bible, the Square and Compasses, and the entire lodge and its officers standing in solemn stillness. He has become an Entered Apprentice Mason. Along with his blindfold, the cable tow is removed from his neck. He can now be symbolically trusted to govern himself without any coercion.

The Recapitulation. The name for this part of the ceremony is self-explanatory. The Candidate—now addressed as "Brother" since he has now become a Mason— receives a lecture from the conferring officer detailing the reasons for the ceremony he has undergone. The petitioning system is narrated and explained. Voting procedures in the lodge are revealed to him. It is emphasized that Freemasonry is an exclusive honor and that high personal standards are expected of the new member. The reason he is wearing only one slipper is explained. It is supposed to commemorate an ancient custom in Israel when promises were exchanged and solemn oaths taken.[27]

After the lecture is over, the conferring officer[28] approaches the new Brother and teaches him the step, sign, password, and the handshake of an Entered Apprentice Mason. He tells him the history of the step and sign and what they are named for. Finally, the procedures for entering and leaving an open lodge meeting are outlined. He then directs the new Brother to go with his Guide back to the Preparation Room, where he will change into his normal clothes, and then reenter the lodge room for further instruction and ceremony.

The Investiture. After being taken back into the Preparation Room and changing his clothes, the new Brother is led by his Guide to the North East corner of the lodge room, near the Secretary's desk. He climbs the first step of the platform there and is met by the Worshipful Master, who invests him with his Masonic apron. He is taught how to wear it as an Entered Apprentice.

---

[27] *Holy Bible, KJV*, Wichita: Heirloom Bible Pub, 1988. Ruth 4:7.
[28] The brother who gives the Degree and runs the ceremony is temporarily the Worshipful Master of the lodge during the ritual. He wears all the garb and accoutrements of the office. After the Degree is completed, he is relieved by the actual, serving, Worshipful Master.

He is told that it is one of the most ancient of symbols and that nothing is more honorable than for a man to have the right to wear it proudly. He is told about the significance of the working tools of an Entered Apprentice: the common gavel, and the twenty-four- inch gauge. The twenty-four-inch gauge is to remind us that there are only twenty-four hours in a day and they must be used wisely. We owe duties to God, to our fellow man, and to ourselves—especially our families. We must try to balance all of those duties. The common gavel is used by masons to trim stones so that they can be used in a building. We are reminded that we should be polishing our own souls and characters. We are not individuals only; we are part of something bigger and far more important. The Great Architect created us for a purpose, and that purpose involves working with others and creating something larger than ourselves.

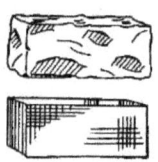

The Charge. We now come to the final stage of this degree. Still standing in the North East Corner, the new Entered Apprentice is given one final lecture by the Master in which he is instructed and charged with meeting certain responsibilities as a Mason.

He is reminded of the ancient and honorable history of Freemasonry and that he is expected to conform to its noble ideals. Some of the world's greatest men did not find it beneath their dignity to join the Fraternity and "level" themselves with their brethren and "act upon the square."

He is told that all monotheistic religions are welcome within the lodge and that religious disputes will not be tolerated. The Great Architect of the Universe does not care what church you belong to, he cares about your heart, and your actions here on earth.

As a citizen, a Freemason is to be a loyal and peaceable member of society. He is to engage in charity and benevolence and not be content with doing nothing while there is suffering he can help to alleviate or perhaps remedy.

He is to behave as a gentleman in the lodge—in the complete sense of that term. He is to treat our ceremonies with the respect that is due them. He is never to mar the harmony and good order of his lodge through jealousy, or a lack of seriousness.

He is to obey the elected and appointed officers of his lodge. He is not to engage in quarrels with critics and enemies of Masonry. He is to improve himself morally and intellectually. He is to conduct his life in such a way that people will ask: "What motivates that man? What is his secret?"

Finally, he is never to recommend a man to become a Freemason unless he truly believes he is able to meet the moral and spiritual requirements of the Brotherhood.

After this short lecture, the new Entered Apprentice is welcomed to the lodge, signs the membership book, and is seated with the Brethren on the "sidelines."

Such then, is the First Degree, the Entered Apprentice Mason's Degree. When one takes this Degree, one is said to have been "Entered." Looking back, I've received many Masonic honors. I've climbed the ladder of service in the Fraternity to some of its highest rungs. I've probably undergone thirty or so Masonic initiations of one sort or another. But the high point of my career, and one I always remember first, is this one. I think you will agree as you continue to labor in the "quarries of the craft," that this night is one of the most memorable you will ever experience.

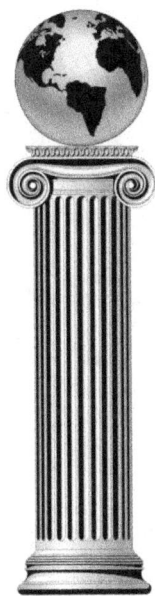 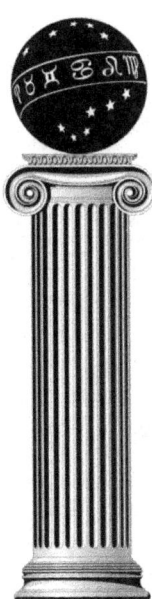

Pillars & Globes: The Temple of Solomon at Jerusalem had two large pillars at its entrance. These have become an important part of Masonic symbolism. Many lodges have pillars in the East. Sometimes they are surmounted by globes. One is the terrestrial, the other the celestial. The terrestrial is more commonly called the earth. The celestial is meant to represent the heavens. They are symbolic of the universality of Freemasonry.

Books Well Worth Reading

I should have titled this list: "Books that *I* think are Worth Reading." Everyone's taste is different. If one investigates, one finds as many lists of Masonic books as there are lists of "Greatest War Movies," or "Best Western Movies." This is simply *my* list. You can agree or disagree. There is no significance as to order.

1. *The Little Masonic Library*, (in 5 Volumes) published by Macoy, Inc.
2. *A Pilgrim's Path*, John J. Robinson.
3. *The Master Builders* Vol. I-III, Wayne A. Huss, pub. by GL of PA.
4. *Living the Enlightenment*, Margaret C. Jacob.
5. *The Freemasons*, Jasper Ridley.
6. *Revolutionary Brotherhood*, Steven C. Bullock.
7. *The Great Teachings of Masonry*, H.L. Haywood.
8. *The Rosslyn Hoax?* Robert L.D. Cooper.
9. *The Exemplar*, Grand Lodge F. & A.M. of Pennsylvania.
10. *Coil's Masonic Encyclopedia*, Henry Wilson Coil.
11. *The Origins of Freemasonry*, David Stevenson.
12. *The Genesis of Freemasonry,* David Harrison.
13. *Schism: The Battle the Forged Freemasonry,* Ric Berman

As I've said, there are a million other books on Masonry, but I'd advise any Brother to start with these thirteen items. Don't fall for all the conspiracy books, or the popular books that claim on the book-jacket to "uncover the shocking truth about…". You can bet that they won't do any such thing. Also, don't feel that you have to read these books right away in order to become a well-informed Brother. Take your time!

5. THE SECOND DEGREE

In Pennsylvania one month must pass before a Candidate takes his Second Degree. There are several reasons for this. First, lodge meetings held for degree conferrals are usually held once a month, so it would be uncommon for a lodge to give two degrees. Second, there are proficiency requirements that must be met before a Brother can receive another degree. In recent years these procedures have been altered by the Grand Lodge, but traditionally, most lodges observe the one-month time period. Finally, custom in our state recommends a period of reflection as a means of helping each man absorb the lessons of the Craft. A month intuitively feels like the right amount of time.

The proficiency requirements are not overwhelming. One must have a "working knowledge" of the Oath and Obligation. What that has meant in practice is that the new Mason must be able to give an account of what the oath is about and what he has promised to do. The sign, password, grip, handshake, and working tools must be familiar to the new Apprentice. That's really all there is to it. Not so long ago the entire Oath and Obligation had to be memorized word-for-word. Each new Mason would be assigned an instructor who would lead him step-by-step through the process. All of the learning was done through oral repetition. Nothing was allowed to be written down. The so-called "mouth to ear" method is still a good one. I would personally recommend it. One gets to know one's instructor very well after a month of working and learning with him. This, in turn, helps one to begin meeting the other members of the lodge, and provides a path to becoming an active member.

In many ways, the Second—the Fellow Craft Degree—is my favorite ceremony. I am in the distinct minority in this view, however. The degree, in certain ways, is the "middle child" of the Masonic ritual. It is the shortest of the three degrees—only about 45 minutes from start to finish. It is the easiest to learn and therefore, the easiest to forget. It is usually treated as an afterthought, even by the Candidate. The First Degree is full of mystery and is the beginning of one's Masonic journey. The Third, or Master Mason's Degree, is the culmination of one's experience in joining the Fraternity. It is the most elaborate of the rituals. The Fellow Craft Degree is usually remembered as just a bridge between the two more memorable ceremonies.

I disagree. What I like about the Fellow Craft ceremony is that it is more relaxed. The Candidate generally knows what to expect. He knows the form of a degree. He has already experienced what it is like to enter, and participate in, a lodge ritual. The nervousness is gone. He can actually relax a little, try to remember his experience, and understand the evening. In addition, the candidate is not "hoodwinked." He is only blindfolded in the opening degree. Now he can see what is going on and enjoy the visual part of the ritual. Like the other Degrees, the Fellow Craft is composed of the same basic parts: the preparation, circumambulation, obligation, recapitulation, investiture, and charge.

The Preparation. This part of the degree process takes little time. The Candidate knows exactly where the Preparation Room is, and he knows much more about what is expected of him. He is usually more comfortable with his Guide and everything goes much more smoothly. Physically and spiritually, he is better prepared than before.

With the help of his Guide, he again removes his clothing and dons his special Candidate's garment. This time, however, his *right* pant leg is rolled up to expose his right knee. He is again barefoot, but a slipper is now worn on his left foot. As before, he has no metal objects or any valuables on his person. The cable tow is now knotted and wound twice around his left upper arm. It is used to tie him to his Guide, but he will not need to be forcefully restrained, since he is already knowledgeable about some of the mysteries of the Craft. When dressed, the Candidate waits with his Guide until the lodge is ready to receive him. He already knows the reasons for his waiting, for his dress, and why he has to wait.

When the proper time comes, the Candidate knocks by himself. He doesn't need assistance. His Guide still speaks for him when the officer enters and enquires about the purpose of his knock. He announces that the Candidate has progressed in his study of the mysteries of Freemasonry, and that he desires to be passed to the Degree of Fellow Craft. After more ceremony and inquiries, as well as giving the password, the Candidate is led into the lodge room.

The Circumambulation. When he enters the lodge room the lights are now turned on. The Candidate can now see what is happening and where he is being led. He circles the Altar two times, stopping twice. He is asked by the two most senior officers of the lodge what his business is this night. His Guide replies that he seeks more "Masonic Light" and wisdom and wishes to be passed to the Degree of Fellow Craft Mason. In both instances, his Guide must give the password for him to proceed. Finally, he is stopped on the Western side of the Altar, told to face the East and advance *two* steps this time, where he kneels before the Holy Bible, Square and Compasses.

The Obligation. This part is also very similar to what was experienced in the previous Degree. In this particular obligation the Candidate repeats much of what he has already promised concerning secrecy. He then makes an additional promise of obedience. He agrees to obey the commands of the lodge, of the officers appointed and elected over him, and also Masonic requests by his fellow Brethren.

As in the First Degree, the oath is sealed with traditional, horrible penalties. He agrees once more that he should die and be horribly mutilated if he breaks his word. Again, before the new Fellow Craft recites his Oath and Obligation, he is reminded by the Worshipful Master that the penalties are traditional only and are not actually enforced. They are metaphors for invoking punishment from heaven if he should prove a liar and break his word. Just as before, the Candidate swears "so help me God," and kisses the Holy Bible—twice this time—to additionally seal himself to the Brotherhood.

The Recapitulation. This part of the ritual is again, much shorter than in the previous Degree. Much that had to be explained before, is now already understood by the Candidate. There is no need to tell him why he wears a special outfit, or one slipper, or why he must not take metal objects into the lodge room. It *is* repeated that he has bound himself to secrecy and now also to obedience.

The self-developmental aspect of Freemasonry is now emphasized to him. He is enjoined to be a lover of the arts and sciences and to educate himself in the Seven Liberal Arts. Traditionally they were divided into grammar, rhetoric, logic, arithmetic, geometry, music, and astronomy.[29] In Masonic symbolism, light is a metaphor for truth and knowledge. All of our rituals and ceremonies revolve around the seeking of differing forms of light. For life to be valuable and rich, we must understand ourselves, our world, the forces of nature, and also the history of mankind. Wisdom is what a man should aspire to, not in order to pose as learned, but in order that he may live a happy and fulfilled life.[30]

---

[29] Henry W. Coil, *Coil's Masonic Encyclopedia,* Richmond, VA: Macoy Publishing & Masonic Supply Co. Inc., 1995, p. 378.

[30] H.L. Haywood, *The Great Teachings of Masonry,* Richmond, VA: Macoy Publishing & Supply Co. Inc., 1986, pp. 141-42.

The Seven Liberal Arts were so named because the Romans believed that they encompassed the proper course of study for a "free" man. Other studies, involving the learning of skills or trades, were for professional purposes. They enabled a man to earn a living. The Liberal Arts gave him a *reason* and *purpose* for living.

Does this mean that Masons are all busy taking extension courses at the local college? Are they required to read a book every week? Of course not. Modern life has to be balanced, and not everyone has the time, or the inclination, to become an amateur academic. What this *does* mean however, is that every Freemason has a serious responsibility to grow intellectually in some way on a regular basis. All Brethren are aware of their Oath and make an honest effort to try to fulfill their obligation. As you stretch your mind in the future, you will find the process rewarding and also a cause for pride and self-confidence.

Finally, the Candidate is shown the step, sign, grip, and handshake of a Fellow Craft Mason. He is also given the password. Their origin and significance are explained. He is told how to enter, and leave, a lodge of Fellow Craft Masons. As before, he is sent out of the lodge room to change into his original clothing and return for further instruction.

The Investiture. As in the previous degree, the new Fellow Craft is led by his Guide to the North East corner of the lodge, near the Secretary's desk. He climbs to the second step of the platform there and is met by the Worshipful Master who invests him with his Masonic apron. He is taught how to wear it in the fashion of a Fellow Craft Mason. He, of course, already knows about the significance of the apron from the previous lecture.

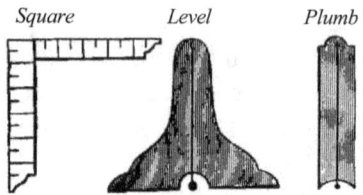

Square   *Level*   *Plumb*

Next, the working tools of a Fellow Craft Mason are explained to him. They are (right to left): the plumb, the level, and the square. The plumb is a tool used by working masons to make sure that perpendicular lines are correct. The level is used to make sure that horizontals are in alignment. The square is to make sure that corners are truly at 90-degree angles. These tools are obviously of value when building a structure. He is shown that these tools remind Freemasons to be proud and walk uprightly in their lives, doing what is good and right. A brother should meet his fellows "on the square," treating everyone he meets with honesty and justice. Finally, he is reminded, that all of us are making a journey on the level of time. That journey will end someday and, when we reach our destination, we will have to answer for our actions during this life.

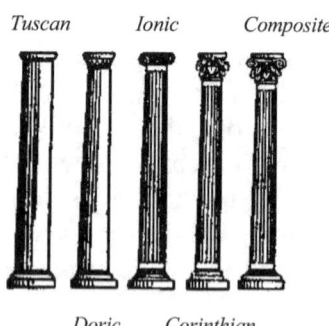

Tuscan   *Ionic*   *Composite*

Doric   *Corinthian*

Next, the Candidate is instructed concerning the five classical orders of architecture: the Tuscan, Doric, Ionic, Corinthian, and Composite. These orders were invented by the ancient Greeks and Romans. The Tuscan is the plainest, least adorned order, the Composite the most elaborate. Each was used to build a unified, symmetrical structure. If you look around, you can easily see their influence to this day on our buildings. Freemasons are still builders, but we expend our energy building a spiritual temple: our character, and our soul. Choose wisely when constructing your spiritual self. Don't just use odds and ends that come to hand. Have a plan and carry it through. As each order of architecture has a unified conception, so should your individual life plan.[31]

Just as architecture was at one time seen as the search for order amidst chaos, so the Freemason should seek order in his life, in his spirit, and in his intellectual development. The letter "G" is a symbol that is commonly associated with Freemasonry. It is said by many to stand for geometry, which originally was synonymous with Masonry. It also has

G

a religious significance. It, of course, stands for GOD and should always remind us that we are dependent upon the Creator in all things. We should remember to place our faith and trust in The Great Architect of the Universe. Every time you see the Masonic symbol, and what is at its center, this lesson should be reinforced in your mind.

The Charge. We now come to the final stage in the degree. The new Fellow Craft is given a final lecture by the

---

[31] Roberts, pp. 51-2.

Master in which he is instructed and charged with meeting additional responsibilities as is expected of a Mason who has been passed to a higher degree.

First, he is congratulated on his advancement in Freemasonry. He is reminded that he is still being judged upon his character and qualifications to fully enter into the Brotherhood. He has met the tests so far, and has therefore, merited the additional honor of this Degree.

Next, he is again advised to improve himself by polishing his mind and character through the study of the Liberal Arts. Geometry, and its implications for order and design, are earnestly recommended to him. Just as a building depends upon the principles of geometry to stand upright, so a man's character and soul depend on an intelligent design to develop to the fullest. Also, just as a building cannot exist without an architect, so the world is the product of the One Great Architect. He is requested to always remember this fact.

Thirdly, the new Fellow Craft is again warned that he must live up to the standards expected of a Freemason. He is to attend lodge faithfully, to treat its ceremonies and customs with respect and veneration, and induce others to do the same.

Finally, he is reminded of his oath of obedience which has formed such a large section of the Second Degree. He is to obey all requests and summons from his lodge, and from his fellow Masons, when duly received from the proper Masonic authority.

Such then, is the Second Degree, the Fellow Craft Mason's Degree. It is a short ceremony, but one which is packed with symbolism and lessons. If you get a chance to participate in one in the future, treat it with the importance that it deserves. As I've said before, it is a small Degree, but it can be pivotal in a Masonic career. Each ritual, if done badly or carelessly, will leave an indelible, poor impression on the new member. After suffering through a mediocre degree, it's hard to get that bad taste out of one's mouth. Some men never can. Remember, each degree that you witness, or participate in, is the most important degree ever—at least to the Candidate. Never forget that. Put yourself in his place when you are tempted to laugh or joke during the ritual. And also, remember your Oath and Obligation from this degree, and your own promise to refrain from treating the Masonic mysteries lightly.

PA Fact: Bro. George M. Dallas was Grand Master in 1835. He refused to testify before a State House Anti-Masonic Investigating Committee in Harrisburg, and his statement before it was published and became a Masonic classic. Dallas was U.S. Secretary of the Treasury under James Madison in 1814, Mayor of Philadelphia in 1828 and, in 1831, a U.S. Senator. President Van Buren appointed Dallas Ambassador to Russia in 1837. His highest post was Vice-President under James K. Polk (1845-49). While in office, Texas was admitted as a state—partly due to his efforts in the Senate. In gratitude, Texas named a city after him.[32]

---

[32] Huss, Vol. III. pp. 111-114.

6. THE THIRD DEGREE

The Third Degree is officially known in Pennsylvania as the Sublime Degree of Master Mason. It is the highest Degree, and the highest honor, that a Freemason can achieve. There are many other Masonic groups and bodies that give degrees with larger numbers—the most notable being the Scottish Rites' 32nd Degree. Many outsiders (the *profane*), mistakenly believe that these degrees are somehow superior, and that being awarded them makes one a more "important" Mason. This is a very large misconception. These other bodies are worth joining, but after receiving the Sublime Degree of Master Mason, one has achieved the pinnacle in Freemasonry. We will cover these other "Appendant" groups in another chapter, but suffice to say right now, that membership in all of them is contingent upon one's being a Master Mason in good standing.

After the customary period of one month, during which time knowledge proficiency is achieved for the new Fellow Craft, the Master Mason's Degree is ready to be conferred. By this time, the Candidate has a very good idea of what will happen to him, and how he is to be prepared for the ritual. At this point, a final series of revelations are revealed. As in other areas of life, just when you think you know it all, surprises spring up. The Third Degree is much more elaborate than the first two. It is the longest degree, taking around two hours to complete. It has another section in it that the other Degrees do not have. In this ceremony some mysteries in the previous degrees are explained. Words, actions, and phrases that were obscure until this point are illuminated for the Candidate. Finally, the purpose and meaning, as well as the birth of the Brotherhood, are revealed. It's a memorable evening, to say the least. After the experience, I remember being dazed for a week, trying to piece together the entire initiation, and figure out the significance of what I had just undergone.

The Preparation. As in the Fellow Craft Degree, the Candidate arrives relaxed and confident. He feels that he knows what will happen and is usually looking forward to finishing his Masonic journey and becoming a full-fledged Mason. As soon as he enters the Preparation Room however, things start to take a slightly unexpected turn. After removing his clothes and his personal possessions, he finds that his Candidate's costume is significantly different than before. It now consists only of the trousers. He is bare-chested. Both of his pant legs are rolled up so that his knees are bare. No slippers are worn. He is barefoot. The cable tow is now wound three times around his waist. Already cold, and a little embarrassed, he knocks on the door to the lodge three times and lets his Guide answer the now familiar questions as to his purpose this night.

The Circumambulation. When he enters the body of the open lodge, he is led by his Guide only once around the Altar, stopping in front of the Worshipful Master who asks why he is here? His Guide replies that he seeks still more "Masonic Light" and wisdom. He wishes to be further instructed in the mysteries of Freemasonry and be raised to the Sublime Degree of Master Mason. His Guide gives the proper password. Then he is taken to the Western side of the Altar, told to face the East and take *three* steps. He kneels before the Altar, lays his hands upon the Holy Bible, Square, and Compasses, and takes the Oath and Obligation of a Master Mason.

The Obligation. In this particular obligation the Candidate once again repeats much of what he has already promised concerning secrecy and obedience. He also agrees to perform many other additional duties. It is the longest of the three obligations by far. He agrees to support and obey the rules and regulations of his lodge and also of the Grand Lodge of Pennsylvania. He agrees to support and defend all Brother Master Masons. He also promises to be charitable to all people, but especially to fellow Brethren. He agrees to uphold the Masonic traditions of morality, good character, belief in a Creator, and also swears to follow the traditional Masonic rules against letting underage men, those of unsound mind, or women join the Fraternity.

As in the other Degrees, the oath is sealed with traditional, horrible penalties. He agrees that his body should be torn apart, burned, and the ashes scattered, if he breaks his word. Again, before promising this, he is reminded by the Worshipful Master that the penalties are traditional only and are not actually enforced. And finally, just as is the previous Degrees, the Candidate swears "so help me God," and kisses the Holy Bible—three times now—to additionally seal himself to the Brotherhood.

The Recapitulation. This part is also very similar to the previous Degrees. The Worshipful Master goes over the entire ritual up to this point and explains the significance of the actions the Candidate was instructed to perform. For example, his bare feet are intended to remind him of the story of Moses and the burning bush. God commanded Moses to remove his sandals in his presence.[33] The reason he entered the lodge room shirtless, was to prove that he was

---

[33] *Holy Bible,* Exodus 3:2-6.

not a woman, for only males are allowed to join the Fraternity.

After these preliminaries, the Worshipful Master goes over the step, sign, password, and handshake of a Master Mason. Their origin and significance are explained. The Candidate is also told how to enter and leave a lodge of Master Masons. At this point, however, the Degree changes. Instead of returning to the Preparing Room and changing into his regular clothes, the Worshipful Master does not let go of the Candidate's hand. Instead, he conducts him to the East, directly in front of the station of the Master, at the foot of the three steps of the raised platform.

Lecture in the East. It is now that the Candidate realizes that the ritual has changed radically and that this will not be the familiar experience that he has gone through before. Still standing half-naked in the East, he is now the sole recipient of an oration by the Master which details the origins of the Craft.

The lecture deals with the legend of the death of Hiram Abiff and the building of the Temple at Jerusalem by King Solomon. It is unclear when this story entered Masonic lore. The first published reference to it is contained in James Anderson's 1723 work, *The Constitutions of the Free-Masons.*[34] The allusion is fairly cryptic however. Only much later in the 1700's did the tale become a basic element within the ritual.[35]

---

[34] Facsimile reprint in *The Little Masonic Library, Book I*, Richmond, VA: Macoy Publishing & Supply Co., Inc., 1977, pp. 159-274.

[35] Since Masonic secrecy has always been a priority, it is almost impossible to trace the development of the ritual during this period. Such clues as we have are due to the existence of Masonic "*exposés,*" in which critics of the fraternity published pirated versions of the ritual. One of the earliest of these works was anonymously published in Dublin, Ireland in 1777. Entitled *M*h*b**e, or The Grand Lodge Door Open'd*, it has been republished in facsimile form by Kessinger Publishing Company, Kila, MT, 2006.

The skeleton of the story is found in the Holy Bible in I Kings, 6-8, and in II Chronicles, 2-7. King David, after unifying the Hebrew tribes and creating the Kingdom of Israel, wished to crown his reign by building a temple to Jehovah in the city of Jerusalem. For a variety of reasons, he could not accomplish this aim and contented himself with gathering materials for the project. He left it to his son and successor, King Solomon to carry out his ambition. Solomon realized that his small country lacked the necessary architects and builders, so he asked an ally, King Hiram of Tyre for help. Hiram gladly supplied additional materials and also expert planners, and craftsmen. One of these builders was named Hiram Abiff.[36] With the help of this master craftsman, and other aid supplied by the Tyrians, the Temple at Jerusalem was completed and dedicated by King Solomon. Such is the story found in the Holy Bible.

Masonic lore contains additional elements not found within the biblical record. According to this version, King Solomon of Israel, King Hiram of Tyre, and Hiram Abiff jointly planned and built the temple. They each took the title of "Grand Master" and presided over thousands of Masters, Fellow Crafts, and Apprentices while the construction of the temple was proceeding.

When the project was almost finished, the three Grand Masters decided that the most worthy of the Fellow Crafts would be promoted to the status of Master so that they could travel about the world and earn their living on their own. In order to prove their credentials, they would be given the secret password, sign, and handshake of a Master Mason. These honors could only be given by the three

---

[36] No satisfactory translation of the surname "Abiff" has been discovered. Some Biblical scholars feel that it can be taken to mean "the widow's son," some editions of the Bible simply include it as a meaningless name or title.

Grand Masters together since they had sworn an oath to heaven to only reveal the words and signs jointly.

Word of the promotions soon leaked out among the workmen. Fifteen Fellow Crafts decided to steal the credentials of a Master, since they did not feel they would merit them on their own. Twelve lost their nerve but three decided to carry out their plan. They ambushed Hiram Abiff one morning as he was leaving the temple where he conducted morning devotions alone before planning the day's work. They stationed themselves at the east, west, and southern gates of the temple and demanded the word and sign of a Master. Hiram refused three times, and after being attacked by each Fellow Craft in turn, was finally killed by the last one with a blow from a heavy setting maul.

The three Fellow Crafts then buried his body and fled in shame and terror over their deed. The next day, the crime was revealed, and the plot uncovered by King Solomon and King Hiram. Aside from the horror of the murder itself, the two Grand Masters realized that the secret word and sign of a Master Mason was now lost forever. The three of them had sworn to confer it jointly, and since one of them was dead, they now could never reveal it to anyone else. The twelve Fellow Crafts who had lost their nerve confessed and were sent to find the three murderers. They were soon found and speedily brought back before King Solomon, who passed judgment upon them. Later, the twelve were sent to find the location where the body of Hiram Abiff was buried and hidden.

The corpse was eventually found because the murderers had marked the grave with a sprig of acacia. It was dug up and the first words spoken were adopted as the secret word of a Master Mason. Likewise, the hand clasp used to pull the body out of its grave became the grip of a Master Mason.

As the lecture proceeds to the story of Hiram Abiff's murder, the Candidate's role changes from listener to participant in the tale. As the story of the murder in the temple is outlined, the Candidate is led around the lodge floor and realizes that he is now standing in for the murdered master. He is also symbolically buried and then found. It is a powerful experience. This part of the ceremony ends with the Candidate receiving the Adopted Secret Word of a Master Mason and the accompanying grip. After this part of the ritual, the Candidate is sent back to the preparation room with his Guide in order to change back into his own clothes.

The Investiture. As in the previous Degrees, the new Master Mason is led by his Guide to the North East corner of the lodge, near the Secretary's desk. He now climbs to the third step of the platform and is met by the Worshipful Master who invests him with his Masonic apron. He is taught how to wear it in the proper fashion of a Master Mason.

He is told that the working tools of a Master Mason are all of the ones from the previous degrees. There is a new one however, the trowel. He is reminded that, as real workmen use the trowel to spread cement, Freemasons use the trowel to remind themselves to spread brotherly love and affection among each other, and among mankind in general.

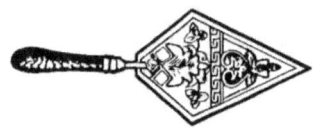

Next, the duty of helping others, especially fellow Freemasons, is outlined. Antique signs of distress, and their accompanying code words, are given to the new member of the lodge. He is reminded that he has a duty as a Freemason—and as a human being—to help everyone as much as he can.

The Charge. We now come to the final stage in the Degree. The new Master Mason is congratulated on his latest achievement. He is now a full-fledged member of the Fraternity. He has no more tests to meet, no more rituals to undergo. He has arrived. He is reminded however of the additional promises he has made during this Degree. All the previous agreements promising obedience and secrecy still are in force. Additionally, the new Freemason is charged with helping his Brethren if they should fall into error. He is also reminded to uphold the traditions and laws of his individual lodge, the Grand Lodge of Pennsylvania, and of any other Masonic organization under whose authority he may find himself.

He is reminded that he is now a full member of his lodge. He is now privileged to speak, to vote, and to propose other men for membership in the Fraternity. He is to always remember the sacred trust that has been placed in him by his Brethren. He is to conduct himself always as a gentleman and to remember that he represents Freemasonry wherever he goes. He is to help all people, but especially fellow Freemasons, and is never to knowingly hurt a Brother in any way. Finally, he is congratulated once more, shakes hands with the Master, and takes his seat with the rest of the Brethren.

In many lodges there are additional little customs and ceremonies at this point. Often a Masonic lapel pin is presented to the new Mason, or sometimes a relative or friend will give him a ring. In my own lodge the new Brother is presented with the Bible that was used in all of his Degrees. There are pages inside for his name, the dates of his Degrees, and the names of the conferring officers. There is also space for all of the attendees to sign. The Brother who signs his application and recommends him for membership normally buys this gift. After additional greetings and congratulations, the newly raised Brother is asked to say a few words. Afterwards, the entire lodge adjourns for a meal together.

Such then, is the Third Degree, the Sublime Degree of Master Mason. It is a night that no Mason can ever forget, and will furnish food for thought for the rest of his fraternal life.

PA Fact: As a Pennsylvania Freemason, you have certain rights as a member. You, or your family, has the right to request a Masonic funeral service for you. If there is a Masonic complaint lodged against you, you have the right to a trial by your peers. You have the right to speak in lodge, to vote, and to hold office. You may petition to change lodges if you move. Dual membership is also allowed subject to Grand Lodge Regulations. You have the right to visit other Pennsylvania lodges, subject to being examined. Always have an up-to-date dues card in your wallet so that you can prove Pennsylvania membership. This privilege includes Prince Hall lodges. Finally, you have the right to Masonic relief and charity. You can ask for help from another Brother or from your lodge. The Masonic Villages is a charitable arm of the Grand Lodge and is open to Master Masons and their families. As with lodge membership, residents must be able to bear the individual cost of the residence program.

"Father is Brother After Son Confers Degrees"

It was a special night for the Burtt family in Harmony Lodge No. 429, Zelienople, when the father became a brother. Robert E. Burtt, Jr., P.M. (second from left), conferred the Master Mason's degree on his father, Robert E. Burtt, Sr. (second from right). The son also had conferred his father's Entered Apprentice and Fellow Craft degrees. "They were the toughest degrees I've ever conferred," he said, "but I'm very proud to be able to call my father 'brother.'" With the Burtts are William M. Baxter, W.M. (left), and S. Robert Marziano, Jr., D.D.G.M., 26th Masonic District.

One never knows what will happen during one's Masonic journey—or during a meeting! That's one reason to keep attending lodge.

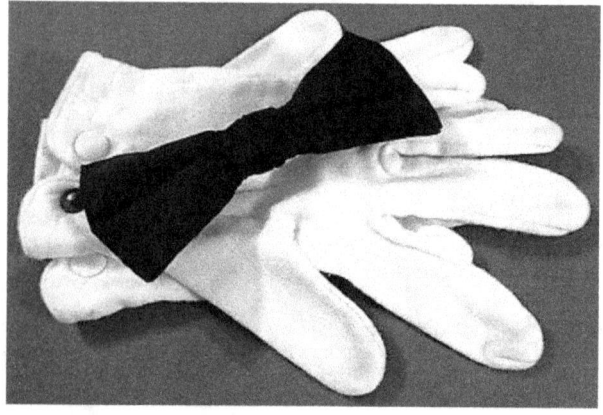

Black bow-tie and white gloves. Part of the wardrobe of the
well-dressed Pennsylvania Freemasons. The tie is part of formal dress.
The white gloves remind the Mason that his hands—and heart—should
be pure at all times.

PART III

TAKE A THIRD STEP FORWARD:

MASONIC LIFE

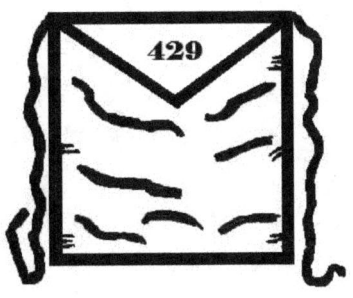

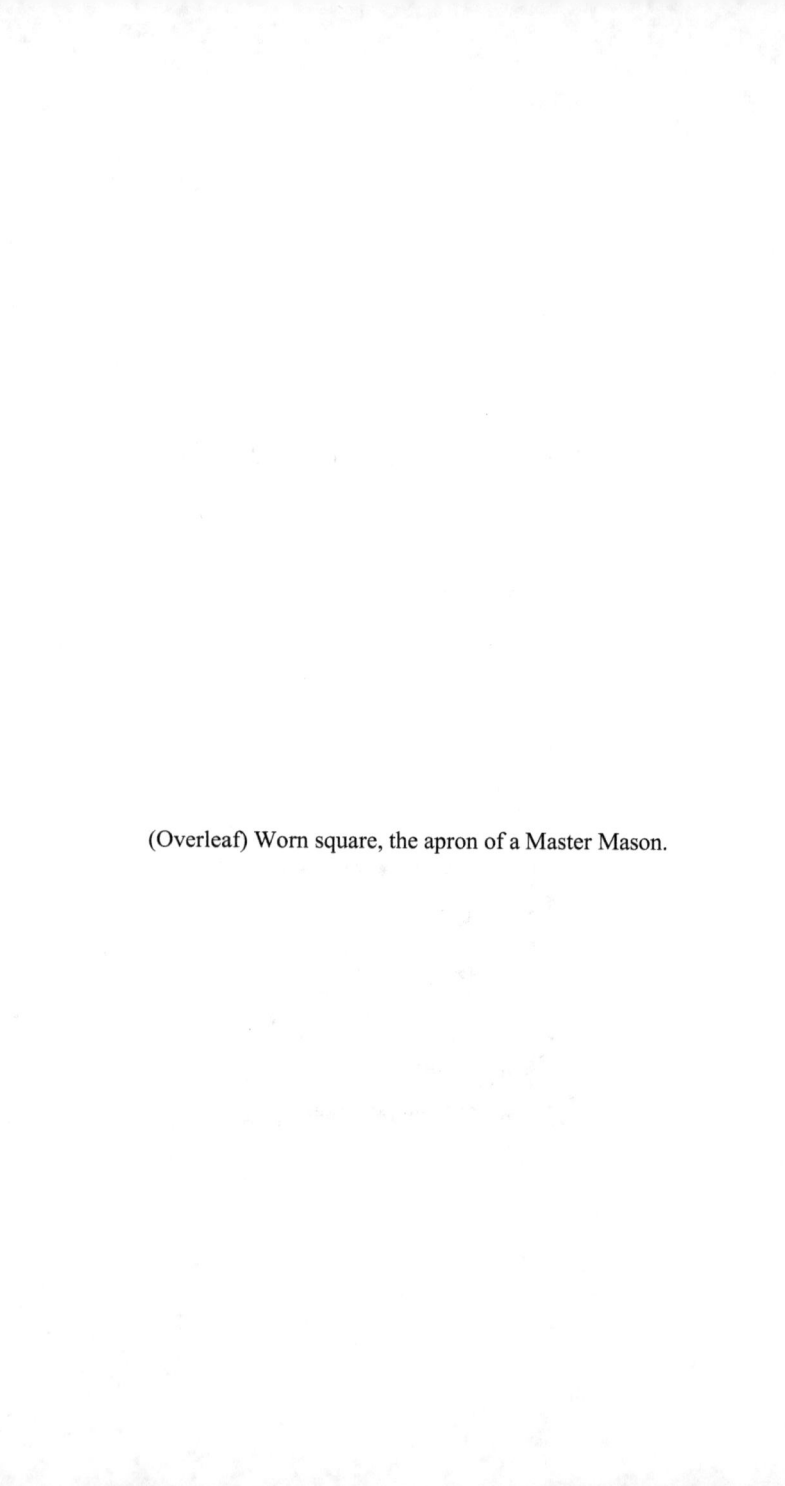

(Overleaf) Worn square, the apron of a Master Mason.

7. HISTORY OF THE GRAND LODGE

The Eighteenth Century: Birth and Independence

As with much of Masonic history, the origins of the Grand Lodge of Pennsylvania are unclear. Like European Masonry, the historical record is incomplete, and does not logically fit together with what we can prove. What we *do* know is that English Freemasonry officially began in June of 1717, and that the Grand Lodge of England began to take formal control of all existing lodges in England and its colonies. This was a legalistic process that involved issuing warrants[37] and asserting the authority of the Grand Lodge.

All of which leads us to Pennsylvania's story. The first Masonic reference concerning our State is found in a document, dated June 5, 1730, issued by the Grand Lodge of England to Daniel Coxe, who was one of the leading Proprietors of the Colony of New Jersey. Coxe was appointed Provincial Grand Master for New York, New Jersey, and Pennsylvania. He was authorized to appoint Junior Provincial Officers, warrant lodges, and in general, set up a perpetuating Masonic Grand Lodge system in America.[38] As in the history of England's Grand Lodge, there is evidence that Freemasonry was already well established in the Keystone state. One Philadelphia lodge, St. John's No. 1, has a constitution that is dated 1727. The *Pennsylvania Gazette* around this time-frame carried news of Masonic proceedings in England which seems to indicate that there were newspaper readers interested in such

---

[37] As mentioned before, a warrant is a document issued by a competent Masonic authority authorizing a lodge to meet and confer Degrees. Any group that meets without such a warrant is technically holding an illegal meeting. It is a "clandestine" group. In the 1700's when Freemasonry was just beginning, many lodges met without such warrants, or felt that they did not need anyone's permission. As Freemasonry became more institutionalized however, that thinking became much more rare. With a few small exceptions, no one has attempted to start a lodge in Pennsylvania without the proper authority in the last 150 years.

[38] Huss, *Volume I*, p. 16.

events.[39] In December of 1730, Benjamin Franklin, the paper's publisher, wrote an article mentioning the fact that several Masonic lodges were active in the city.[40] Finally, one might ask: why would the Grand Lodge of England issue a document to someone in order to establish its Masonic authority, if there weren't good reasons for doing so? Daniel Coxe had to have been a Freemason, and he had to have been an important one, to receive such an authorization. There also had to have been so many lodges meeting in the three colonies mentioned, that the English Grand Lodge felt that it *had* to regulate such activity. In any case, Pennsylvania has the oldest, recorded Masonic activity in existence, and its claims to be the senior Grand Lodge in the United States are secure.[41]

Benjamin Franklin became an important figure in Pennsylvania Freemasonry. When he first wrote about the Fraternity, he was not a Brother. In fact, the article originally contained some pirated ritual exposés and was somewhat satirical in tone. It is possible that he used his influence as a newsman to obtain membership. At this time, Freemasonry was an exclusive, high-toned organization that only the "best" men were allowed to join. Franklin did not qualify in terms of breeding and social standing.

Philadelphia's Masonic community probably reasoned that Franklin was a man on the rise, and that it was better to have him as a member than as an enemy. He became a Freemason in February of 1731. After Franklin's joining the Craft, the *Gazette*'s coverage became much more positive.

In 1732, he drafted a set of by-laws for St. John's Lodge No. 1, and also became Junior Grand Warden of the Grand Lodge of Pennsylvania. His swift rise continued.

---

[39] Ibid, p. 17.

[40] Coil, *A Comprehensive View of Freemasonry*, p. 137.

[41] Secure unless new documentary evidence is unearthed in the future. At the present time, this seems unlikely.

In June, 1734 he was elected Grand Master and printed the first American edition of James Anderson's *Constitutions of the Freemasons*. Franklin also served several times as Secretary of St. John's Lodge, and as Deputy Grand Master.[42]

Pennsylvania's Masonic influence was great during the colonial period. Although the Grand Lodge of England soon issued other dispensations to various colonial grand lodges, Pennsylvania was given great independence and wide powers in its charter. Its Grand Lodge officers could be chosen by the members without the approval of the "Mother country." It also had the authority to warrant lodges anywhere it chose—not just within the confines of the colony.[43] It took advantage of this prerogative and created lodges in Delaware, Maryland, and Virginia.

In June of 1737, the first recorded instance of anti-Masonic public sentiment in America occurred in Philadelphia. An apothecary named Jones, along with two accomplices, played a practical joke on an apprentice by pretending to initiate him into Masonry. The boy died as the result of the hoax, with charges and accusations leveled against the Fraternity. It was felt that Freemasonry was too exclusive and simply a way for elites in society to make everyone else feel inferior. Franklin felt obliged to publish a defense of Freemasonry's rituals, and even had to explain his

---

[42] Huss, *Volume III: Grand Master Biographies*, p. 15.

[43] An interesting side note dealing with this authority concerns Bro. George Washington's Alexandria Lodge No. 22. In 1782 brethren living in Alexandria, VA petitioned the Grand Lodge of Pennsylvania for a charter in spite of the fact that the Grand Lodge of Virginia had been in operation since 1778. The charter was granted and the lodge opened under Pennsylvania's authority as lodge No. 39! A few years later, during an administrative reorganization within the Grand Lodge, the Alexandria Lodge was given its Masonic freedom. It thereupon decided to petition the Grand Lodge of Virginia for a new charter. It was granted and George Washington became its first Worshipful Master. Carl H. Claudy, *Washington's Home and Fraternal Life*, Silver Spring, MD: Masonic Service Association, 1981. pp. 35-7.

membership to his parents in Boston a year later. The fact that Jones was not himself a Mason did little to satisfy the public. The Grand Lodge felt obliged to publicly disassociate itself from the incident and stopped publishing Masonic news in Franklin's Philadelphia newspaper.

The incident highlighted an important division within Freemasonry that became increasingly serious as the 18th Century wore on: the conflict between the "Moderns," and the "Ancients." As previously mentioned, the Grand Lodge of England was formed on June 24, 1717 in London. This event was the culmination of a long process that brought Freemasonry into being. Anthony Sayer was elected Grand Master. Little is known about him except that he was titled "Gentleman" in the official minutes. This fact seems to indicate that, while Sayer was a committed and respected Freemason, he had little prestige or status within London society.[44]

In an effort to increase its popularity and *cachet*, the Grand Lodge began accepting members of the nobility as Brethren. On June 24, 1721, Lord Stanhope, the Earl of Chesterfield was made a Mason and the Duke of Montague was chosen Grand Master. In 1723, the Duke of Wharton assumed office. Under the leadership of aristocrats such as these, members with less exalted backgrounds felt left out. Complaints began to be aired about declining standards for membership. Ritualistic work soon became neglected. Freemasonry seemed to be in danger of turning into a rich man's drinking club. By 1738, under the leadership of Lord Byron, the Craft seemed headed for oblivion.[45]

It was during this period that an insurgent movement arose in London which was to transform the Fraternity. In 1751, Laurence Dermott, an Irish businessman, formed

---

[44] Coil, *A Comprehensive View of Freemasonry*, pp. 69-70.
[45] Ibid, pp. 72-81.

"The Grand Lodge of Antient Masons" in London. Charging that the current Grand Lodge had wrongly instituted "Modern" changes to ritual and customs, he led a revival to restore purity and equality to Masonry.

Most of Dermott's charges were true. Ritual *was* being neglected, and the organization *was* becoming too elitist in its membership. "Antient" Masonry aimed to restore the Craft to its original form and intent. As part of this effort, Dermott published a new handbook of rules and regulations to replace James Anderson's *Constitutions*. He called his book the *Ahiman Rezon*, sometimes translated as "Help to a Brother."[46] The work was much less flowery than Anderson's and was more practical and clearly written.

The movement spread through the Masonic world like wild-fire and membership soared among the newly emerging middle-class. The Ancient Grand Lodge also instituted some innovations like "military lodges." They were formed within British Army regiments, and spread Freemasonry throughout the Empire. Soon even the original Grand Lodge had given up and began calling itself the "Modern" form of Masonry. By 1813, the battle was over. The two Grand Lodges merged and became "The United Grand Lodge of Ancient Freemasons of England." With this internecine war over, Freemasonry became mostly middle-class, and much stricter—ritualistically speaking.

The Pennsylvania "Ancient" Masonic movement mirrored the concerns of Brethren—and would-be Brethren—in England. The first lodge was organized in 1757 and it steadily overcame the already established "Modern" Grand Lodge. Offering membership to groups outside the social elite, and preserving Masonry's identification with cosmopolitan culture, proved an irresistible combination to the "middle class." When

---

[46] Ibid, p. 108.

Benjamin Franklin left for England in 1757, he was one of the leading Freemasons in Pennsylvania. When he returned home in 1785, he no longer could enter a lodge. The Grand Lodge he had once headed no longer existed![47] Indeed, one of the dirty little secrets of Pennsylvania Masonry is that, when he died in 1790, Franklin did not receive a Masonic funeral—he was not a member in good standing of any Philadelphia lodge! The Grand Lodge of Free and Accepted Masons (Ancients), did not participate in any organized ceremony mourning his death.

Fortunately, Franklin's Masonic career in Europe bore positive fruits for his country. As U.S. representative to the French Court during the Revolution, he was able to use his status as a Mason to influence royal officials and obtain recognition and aid for the rebellious colonies. His entrée into Masonic circles in France was vital in this effort. Aside from Washington, Franklin played the most important role in the War for Independence.

At home in Philadelphia, the Grand Lodge officially played a neutral role during the Revolution. The same could not be said for many of its subordinate lodges. Six lodges in the city, and its surrounding counties, produced over 250 officers for the Continental Army. Many lodges took public stands supporting the rebellion and raised money and supplies for the cause.[48] When the British Army departed Philadelphia in 1778, a great Masonic celebration was held on St. John's Day, December 28. Over three hundred Masons participated in a procession through the city, led by General George Washington. Church services, musical programs, and dinners at several lodges in the city concluded

---

[47] Steven C. Bullock, *Revolutionary Brotherhood: Freemasonry and the Transformation of the American Social Order, 1730-1840*, Chapel Hill, NC: University of North Carolina Press, 1996. pp. 85-90.
[48] Huss, Vol. I, pp. 30-31.

the largest Masonic public ceremony ever held up to that time. The Fraternity also increased its prestige through its association with Washington.[49]

With the Revolution won, and political independence achieved for the new United States, the Grand Lodge of Pennsylvania declared its own independence from the Grand Lodge of England. On March 27, 1786 it declared "That this Grand Lodge is, and ought to be . . . Independent of Great Britain or any other Authority whatever . . ."[50] With no animosity, it sent a letter to the Grand Lodge of England informing it of the break, but asking for mutual recognition and brotherly affection as an equal. Because of confusion over who was actually in charge in England (Moderns or Ancients), a reply was not received until 1792. The Grand Lodge of England then heartily endorsed Pennsylvania's independence and sent its congratulations and affection.

Throughout the 1700's, Freemasonry in Pennsylvania grew in membership despite the Moderns-Ancients feud, and the turmoil caused by the Revolution. At the turn of the century, it was well-established in the Commonwealth. There were about 50 lodges scattered throughout the state with around 1,500 brethren (out of a population of 100,000 adult males).[51] The future looked bright for the Fraternity.

The Nineteenth Century: Disaster and Resurgence

Through the first quarter of the 1800's, Freemasonry in Pennsylvania, and within the United States, seemed to be experiencing a "Golden Age." By almost every measure the Brotherhood played a dominant role in American civic life. The cornerstone laying ceremonies of the U.S. Capital

---

[49] Ibid, p. 41.
[50] Ibid, p. 57-57.
[51] Numbers are from Huss, Vol. I, pp. 293, 80. Also see U.S. Census data, 1800.

building and the White House were Masonic. Most public buildings across the country were also dedicated with Masonic rites. Most public leaders were Freemasons—at least it seemed so to many observers. In 1824, President James Monroe, Speaker of the House Henry Clay, and Chief Justice John Marshall were all active Masons. At the local level Masonic influence seemed pervasive. The United States could almost have been termed a "Masonic Republic."

Within Pennsylvania, the Fraternity flourished as well. Where before 1785, lodges had mainly been confined to the southeast corner of the State, by 1825 lodges were spread throughout the Commonwealth. Membership rose to about 3,500—double what it had been in 1800.[52] In physical terms, the Grand Lodge successively built larger and more impressive buildings in which to meet. In 1810, a large, elaborate, gothic Grand Lodge Hall was dedicated on Chestnut Street in Philadelphia. It soon became a showplace of the city and attracted much favorable attention for the Fraternity.[53] No one would have predicted that Freemasonry was about to enter an era of crisis.

In western New York State, during the year 1826, occurred a series of events known to history as "The Morgan Affair." William Morgan, a Masonic imposter and ne'er-do- well, attempted to publish an exposé of the ritual. He was arrested on trumped up charges, kidnapped from the county jail, and disappeared. Most local officials were Freemasons. After twenty trials and three Special Prosecutors, only a handful of convictions were obtained. At the very least, obstruction of justice had occurred due to Masonic influence. Public outrage was so great that a new movement was born almost overnight: "Anti-Masonry."[54]

---

[52] Huss, Vol. I, pp. 147, 296.
[53] Ibid, p. 74.
[54] Bullock, pp. 277-278.

The movement embodied two criticisms of Freemasonry that had festered underneath the surface of American society for some time. Many felt that Masonry was elitist and incompatible with the ideals of a free republic. There were also religious objections that it subverted Christianity itself, particularly with its oaths and obligations. The nation could be saved morally and politically only when Freemasonry was utterly destroyed.[55]

Anti-Masonry spread rapidly throughout the United States and was particularly strong in the North. Hundreds of newspapers were founded and a political party created. Candidates won office at all levels running as Anti-Masons. Under public pressure, Freemasons quit the Brotherhood in droves. In Michigan and Vermont, Masonry ceased to operate at all. By the late 1830's, the movement had burned itself out and had merged with other political movements.[56] However, the damage to the Fraternity had been done by then and took years to heal.

Pennsylvania, along with New York, was at the center of the storm. The Anti-Masonic Party held the first-ever national political convention at Philadelphia in 1830. William Wirt, the party's nominee, won a respectable number of votes and gained Vermont's electoral total in the 1832 presidential election. In 1835, Joseph Ritner was elected Governor of Pennsylvania running on the Anti-Masonic ticket. Newly elected state representative Thaddeus Stevens organized a House Committee to Investigate Freemasonry. He failed to obtain subpoena powers, and the authority to obtain written evidence, however. The Committee spent several months trying to investigate Masonry but eventually failed to accomplish anything

---

[55] Ibid, p. 281.
[56] Many members, along with Temperance and anti-slavery activists, Know Nothing's, and Whigs, eventually merged with other groups to form the Republican Party.

because of stubborn refusals by Pennsylvania Freemasons to cooperate in the hearings.[57] Still, the Grand Lodge was held up to public ridicule and contempt, and never recovered its former prestige in society. Membership plunged around the Commonwealth. In 1826 there were 104 lodges in the state with 3,724 members. By 1839, there were only 38 lodges in operation with a membership of 1,761.[58]

The Pennsylvania, leadership of the Grand Lodge made a conscious decision not to engage its critics in a public battle over the merits of Freemasonry. They decided to hunker down, keep losses to membership as low as possible, conserve the finances of the Fraternity, and wait for the storm to pass. Our local customs of secrecy, and of not answering critics, date from this period.

By the 1840's the Grand Lodge was well on its way to recovery. Membership rose steadily through the decade until, by 1855, there were 10,544 brethren in 128 lodges.[59] After the Civil War, Freemasonry experienced a boom period—not only in Pennsylvania, but all over the nation. Clubs, veterans' groups, and civic organizations became very popular in American Society. By 1900, membership in Pennsylvania had reached a total of 65,387 brethren, spread among 436 lodges.[60]

During this period of recovery, two important decisions were made. First, it was decided to invest saved resources into building a new Masonic Temple in Philadelphia for the Grand Lodge. This cemented the city's place as the "Masonic Capital" of the State. Second,

---

[57] Huss, Vol. I, pp. 112-141.
[58] Ibid, pp. 144, 303.
[59] Ibid, pp. 188, 303.
[60] Huss, Vol. II, pp. 62, 208.

Pennsylvania's leaders decided to carve out a unique place for themselves within American Masonry as a whole, and to maintain their independence from the rest of the country.

In 1855 a large, new, Grand Lodge building was dedicated in the western section of Philadelphia on Chestnut St. It was a sumptuous edifice that cost over $180,000—a tremendous sum for its day. In only fifteen years the Fraternity had recovered all of its losses and was once more an accepted public institution. The building soon proved too small, and in 1873 an even larger, more elaborate building replaced it. Located on Broad Street, right beside City Hall, it cost the enormous sum of $1.5 million. It is still the present site of the Grand Lodge of Pennsylvania.[61]

Pennsylvania's Masonic leaders made an even more important decision during this time. In the wake of the Morgan Affair, many pirated rituals and exposés were published. It was felt by many that the ritual was becoming common knowledge. Many Grand Lodges wished to revise Masonic ritual and create a unified Grand Lodge that would have jurisdiction over the entire United States. A convention of fifteen Grand Lodges met in Baltimore, Maryland in May of 1843 to work on these objectives. Pennsylvania refused to attend, or sanction the goals of the convention. The idea of a united Grand Lodge did not receive enough support nationwide, so it never was enacted. A unified system of ritual was devised however, and most states across the country now have degree ceremonies that are similar.[62]

The Grand Lodge of Pennsylvania refused to change its work. To this day, no other state has a ritual like Pennsylvania's. The work in other grand lodges is very

---

[61] Ibid, pp. 183-87, 227.
[62] Ibid, p. 162. Also see, Allen E. Roberts, *Freemasonry in American History*, Richmond, VA: Macoy Publishing & Masonic Supply Co. Inc., 1985. p. 326.

elaborate, complicated, and ponderous. It often features large casts of characters, costumes, singing, prayers, Bible readings, and is somewhat flowery in tone. It perfectly reflects the Victorian Age in which it was adopted. By contrast, Pennsylvania ritual adopted none of these elements. It stayed true to its roots of the 1700's. If one reads old ritual exposés from the 18th Century, it is very similar. It is clear, concise, and short. Much of the language is quaint, but understandable. If you travel around the nation, I think you will agree that the Grand Lodge made a wise decision.

In any case, by the end of the 1800's, the Grand Lodge of Pennsylvania was stronger than it had ever been. It had withstood the storm of Anti-Masonry, had kept its independence, and had grown in membership and influence. It faced the new century with confidence.

The Twentieth Century: Growth and Decline

The Twentieth Century was a roller coaster ride for the Grand Lodge of Pennsylvania. The same could be said for American Freemasonry in general. Masonic growth was steady until it exploded in the period after World War II. Membership in Pennsylvania reached a peak in 1960, but then experienced a steady decline that continues to the present day. The following charts tell the story of the rise and fall of membership in the last one hundred years.

MASONIC MEMBERSHIP
UNITED STATES[63]

Year	Population	Freemasons	Pop	Males
1900	75,994,575	920,459	1.2%	2.4%
1940	131,669,275	2,457,263	1.8%	3.6%
1960	179,323,175	4,099,219	2.3%	4.6%
1990	248,709,873	2,531,643	1%	2%
2000	281,421,906	1,841,169	.7%	1.4%
2012	308,745,538	1,306,539	.4%	.8%
2023	334,233,854	869,429	.26%	.52%

[63] U.S. Department of Commerce, U.S. Census Bureau. "Demographic Trends in the 20th Century: Census 2000 Special Reports." Appendix A, Table 1. "Total Population for the United States, Regions, and States: 1900 to 2000." U.S. Census Bureau, 2002. Web. http://www.census.gov/prod/2020pubs/censr-4.pdf. Masonic Service Association of North America. "Membership Totals since 1924." MSA. Web, 2021. http://www.msana.com/services/jurisdictional-totals/ The Grand Lodge of Pennsylvania, Web, 2012. http://www.pagrandlodge.org/gsecretary/membershiphistory.html.

MASONIC MEMBERSHIP
PENNSYLVANIA

Year	Population	Freemasons	Pop	Males
1900	6,302, 115	65,387	1%	2%
1940	9,900,180	171,851	1.7%	3.4%
1960	11,319,366	257,915	2.2%	4.4%
1990	11,881,643	176,274	1.5%	3%
2000	12,281,054	140,057	1.1%	2.2%
2023	12,961,683	76,313	.59%	1.18%

It would be hard to deny, based on these charts, that Freemasonry seems to be heading towards a grim future. As the era began, the Fraternity in Pennsylvania experienced steady growth and expansion. The pattern of increased membership was interrupted during the years of the Great Depression, but with the Post-War economic boom, the Fraternity experienced a period of growth. Decline then occurred and has continued. To put it mildly, the future seems bleak.

A bright spot was the growth of Masonic Charities, one of the most significant events of the Twentieth Century. In 1908 the goal of a centrally administered Masonic home for the aged and infirm was introduced and work began on the project. On May 25, 1910 the Masonic Home at Elizabethtown was officially opened. Located near the State Capital of Harrisburg, it grew over the years into a state-of-the-art retirement community also open to Pennsylvania Freemasons and their spouses. It has grown to include a state-wide system of homes and facilities for citizens that reaches every part of the state.[64]

Just as economic woes affected membership, other societal factors reached into the lodge and can be seen acting upon us to this day. With the advent of World War I, the flag of the United States began to be displayed in lodge rooms. When Prohibition was instituted during the 1920's, strict regulations concerning alcohol use in lodge buildings were handed down from the Grand Lodge. Lodges are "dry" to this day. During World War II, many lodges began to feature the singing of the National Anthem during meetings, a practice which continues.

Pennsylvania Freemasonry reached its peak in terms of members in 1960. Not only in raw numbers, but in the percentage of males, Masons were a major presence in the Commonwealth. The percentage of males in 1960 was *all* males, not just adults. If adult males were assumed to be, say 40% of the population, it is probable that almost 6% of adult males in Pennsylvania were Freemasons in 1960.

From 1961 on however, each year has shown a decline in membership. For a few decades, there was a difference of opinion among Masonic leaders about how to deal with the problem—or even if declining membership *was* a problem. Demographics was the real culprit, it was

---

[64] Huss, Vol. II, pp. 83-88.

said. Many elderly brethren who had joined in decades past were dying, and the decline was a statistical anomaly which would soon pass as younger men joined and replenished the ranks.

There was also a body of thought that said that too much growth was *bad* for the Fraternity. If membership became common, it would not be valued. Freemasonry, the argument went, was not *designed* to be for every man. It was *supposed* to be exclusive. If the Fraternity was shrinking, so much the better, it was argued. This point of view was often summarized by the slogan: "Not more men into Masonry, but more Masonry into men!"

By the 1980's the decline had become so apparent that the Grand Lodge decided that something *had* to be done. The Grand Lodge instituted a leadership program called "Solomon II" to train lodge officers and address membership loss. This was followed by a campaign to attract members called "Friend to Friend." Since Freemasonry traditionally could not advertise for new members, it was a way to talk about the Fraternity to one's acquaintances in the hopes of attracting new members. These programs, while successful in their way, did not stem the decline in membership in any noticeable way.

More ideas were introduced. The age for becoming a Freemason was lowered from twenty-one to eighteen years. Multiple candidates were allowed to be initiated on the same night. However, the new millennium approached with no permanent solution in sight.

The Twenty-first Century: Renaissance?

As Freemasonry looked toward its Three Hundredth Anniversary in the 2000's, the Grand Lodge decided on a two-pronged approach to membership decline. First, procedures for joining the Fraternity were revamped.

Second, the methods of administration, and some Masonic customs, were modernized.

In the latter part of the 1900's, the requirement that only one man at a time could be initiated into Freemasonry had been changed to allow up to five men to join at one time. In the first decade of the century, more rules were relaxed. So-called "One Day Classes" were instituted in which groups of men could go through all three Degrees in a single day instead of taking up to three months. The method of voting on petitions was modified so that it took three negative "black balls" to reject a candidate, instead of one. Finally, Freemasons were given permission to actively solicit new members by asking them to join.

In every day lodge life and administration, rules were relaxed and modernized. The Grand Lodge allowed electronic notices to be sent over the internet, rather than printing and mailing them the traditional way. Lodges were encouraged to computerize their records and paying dues by credit card was allowed, rather than using old-fashioned checks. Dress standards were relaxed for lodge meetings and the ritual was allowed to be shortened to speed up meetings. Also, the ritual was printed and distributed to lodges to aid in memorization of the material. No longer is "mouth-to-ear" the only method available when learning the work.[65]

It is too soon to know if these reforms will have an effect on the hemorrhaging membership numbers.[66] What *is* important is that the Grand Lodge has recognized the problem and is trying out solutions. My own opinion is that if these innovations don't work, then at least the ice will

---

[65] "Renaissance Q & A with the Grand Master," The Pennsylvania Freemason Vol. LVII, August 2010, No. 3: p. 4.

[66] *Since this work was first published, Pennsylvania experienced positive growth in membership in 2010. The Grand Lodge grew by approximately 4,500 members. As of 2021, however, the gains proved temporary.*

have been broken and other things can be tried. An organization that will *not* try anything new will definitely not solve its problems. Time, as they say, will tell.

The Grand Lodge Today

As a Master Mason and the member of a lodge, you might be curious as to how Pennsylvania is governed in Masonic terms. How is the State organized? The system is fairly straightforward. As mentioned earlier, Philadelphia is the "Masonic Capital" of Pennsylvania and the home of the Grand Lodge. The Grand Lodge of Pennsylvania is set up in a similar way to any "Blue Lodge" in the Commonwealth.

Just as your lodge has a Worshipful Master, Wardens, Deacons, etc., so does the Grand Lodge. Their titles are slightly different, however: "Right Worshipful Grand" is prefaced to every office, as in "Right Worshipful Grand Master, Right Worshipful Grand Senior Warden," and so on. There *is* one extra officer that lodges do not have: The Right Worshipful Deputy Grand Master. He occupies a position between the Grand Senior Warden and the Grand Master.

Grand Lodge officers serve two-year terms and are elected by members of the Grand Lodge. How does one get to be a member of the Grand Lodge? Its membership is made up of all Worshipful Masters in the State, all Past Masters, and all past members of the Grand Lodge. Every quarter there is a meeting of the Grand Lodge where business is transacted and proposals voted on.

Pennsylvania is divided into Masonic Districts, each led by a District Deputy Grand Master. The District Deputy is an appointed officer who serves at the pleasure of the Grand Lodge. A minimum term is five years, with a possible term of up to ten years. Within the District, the Deputy is the voice of the Grand Lodge. Each Masonic district in the state of Pennsylvania is made up of roughly six to ten lodges.

So that's the governing structure: individual Masonic Brother, Lodge, Worshipful Master, Masonic District, District Deputy, Grand Lodge, and Right Worshipful Grand Master.

Many other Grand Lodges have the same forms as Pennsylvania, but they tend to mix overly large elements of democratic governance into the model. Our State uses a republican system which, while giving democracy its due, gives leadership great influence in addressing Masonic concerns and instituting changes.

One of the problems with other states is that many Grand Lodges put major questions to a vote during their quarterly communications. Proxy votes are also allowed so that it is possible to "bundle" absentee members together in order to stop progressive agendas from being passed.

Some Grand Lodges can't even address financial questions since their members consistently vote to keep fees and dues low. Even if a dues increase wins enough votes, it must be approved in consecutive years. In some states, any Brother can run for *any* Grand Lodge office and some elections resemble political campaigns! Pennsylvania combines democracy with republican elements in a conservative structure that has proven to be flexible, responsive, and capable of change.

"You've got to be very careful if you don't know where you are going, because you might not get there."

--Yogi Berra (famous American philosopher)

8. CRITICISMS OF FREEMASONRY

Attacks on Freemasonry are actually older than the organization itself—or at least older than the Grand Lodge of England. In 1698, a handbill was circulated in London condemning that "devilish sect of men…evildoers …corrupt people." It alerted "all godly people in the citie of London" about the "Mischiefs and Evil practiced in the sight of GOD by those called Freed Masons."[67] Remember this was 19 years before the Grand Lodge organized itself in 1717! Assaults on Freemasonry have not stopped since. As a member of the Brotherhood, expect to hear criticisms of our Order in the media, or even among friends and acquaintances. This chapter is meant to outline the basic lines of attack on Masonry and give you some facts should you wish to defend yourself, or the Lodge.

Criticisms of the Fraternity fall into three general categories: religious objections, charges of conspiracy, and imputations of racism. We will deal with each in turn. The vast majority of allegations made against us are nonsense. Some however, have a basis in fact.

Religious Objections

Given that one of Freemasonry's basic beliefs is freedom of personal conscience in religious matters, it is not surprising that organized religion has historically been an enemy of the Brotherhood. I will begin with the Roman Catholic Church and its position concerning our Order. There are several reasons for starting here. First, it is the largest Christian church in the world. Second, it is the oldest, most powerful, and most prestigious denomination. Lastly, it has the longest record of sustained criticisms of Freemasonry.

---

[67] Huss, Vol. I, p. 4.

Soon after Masonry appeared in Europe, the Vatican made its first pronouncement against the Fraternity. In 1737, Pope Clement XII issued a Papal Bull forbidding Catholics to become Masons. Since then, eight popes in seventeen different proclamations have condemned Freemasonry and threatened Catholics with the penalty of excommunication for joining.[68] In 1884, Pope Leo XIII issued *Humanum Genus*, the strongest condemnation of Freemasonry ever issued by the Church, and one that still remains in force today.

In this document, Leo outlined the main issues that the Catholic Church has with the Brotherhood. He charged the Masonic Fraternity with conducting a world-wide conspiracy to undermine and attack the Catholic Church. He complained that the Italian unification of 1870 was the result of a Masonic plot. He also charged Freemasons with being guilty of encouraging *indifferentism*—the belief that all religious beliefs are the same and all are equally valid. *Humanum Genus* also accused Freemasons of belief in the following errors: democratic government, separation of church and state, public schooling, and freedom of conscience![69]

Well, I guess most Freemasons would have to plead guilty to believing in democracy and freedom of religion. The charges of conspiracy are harder to disprove since one would be forced to prove a negative. The facts of history tell us however, that while Garibaldi was a Freemason, the Italian unification movement was not a Masonic plot. Neither Communism nor Fascism were—or are—connected with Freemasonry either.

---

[68] Robert C. Broderick, Ed. *The Catholic Encyclopedia*, New York: Thomas Nelson Publishers, 1987. p. 229.

[69] John J. Robinson, *Born in Blood: The Lost Secrets of Freemasonry*. New York: M. Evans & Co.: 1989. pp. 345-59. This work contains a fair translation of the Latin document. The official Vatican version is wordier, but the meaning is the same.

Things get somewhat complicated for Roman Catholic laymen who might be interested in joining a lodge. In 1974, the Congregation for the Doctrine of the Faith issued a letter stating that Catholic laymen were permitted to join any organization as long as it did not conspire against the Church.[70] Freemasonry was specifically NOT mentioned in this document. This was strange since the specific question it addressed was Masonic membership! In addition, the official Catechism of the Church actually *requires* Catholics to "take an active part in public life... participation may vary from one...culture to another."[71] But then, in 1983, the Congregation issued a new letter restating the Church's old position of forbidding any membership in Freemasonry. This muddied the waters even further.

As a member of the Roman Catholic Church, I would make my case in the following manner. First, Freemasonry is not a religion or a religious organization. It teaches no doctrine of salvation or path to God. It assumes that its members believe in one single deity, but it does not ask for a profession of faith. In fact, religious matters are not spoken of inside the lodge. Second, Freemasonry is a secular organization concerned with charity, self-improvement, and patriotism. In today's world, it actively supports the United States of America, and it assuredly does *not* conspire against the Church. Third, Freemasons *do* believe in freedom of conscience, separation of church and state, and public education. I do not apologize for holding these beliefs. To sum up, most of the Church's accusations are either not true, or invalid as they apply to the Brotherhood. I know this, having been a Freemason for twenty years. Following Cardinal Newman, I claim the supremacy of my own

---

[70] Broderick, p. 375.
[71] *Catechism of the Catholic Church*, The Vatican: 1994. p. 466.

conscience over the authority of the leaders of my church. They have been wrong in the past, and they are wrong in this instance. I bow to their expertise in theology, but not to their political, historical, and philosophical judgments.[72]

Fundamentalism

The Catholic Church is not the only Christian denomination that has attacked Freemasonry. Evangelical fundamentalist ministers have chosen Masonry as a target in recent decades. Many "televangelists" use Freemasonry as a whipping boy. Freemasons are accused of taking "false oaths," or of disobeying the biblical injunction to not swear oaths at all. Masons are also actually accused by some of worshiping the devil. Some fundamentalists accuse the Lodge of setting up its own religion separate from Christianity. They charge Freemasons with ignoring the Christian doctrine of faith through Jesus Christ, and with preaching salvation through good works.

To repeat once again. Freemasonry assumes that one believes in a Supreme Being as a condition of membership. It does not teach a path of salvation and does not recommend

---

[72] Also of note here, is the fact that Vatican doctrine and day-to-day customs and procedures change over the years, leaving the average member of the Church confused. Until the 1960's, Latin was the standard language used during Mass. After Vatican II, vernacular languages were introduced and Latin became a rarity. In recent decades, Vatican policy has been to reintroduce Latin as the language of worship. Another example: in a recent interview, Pope Benedict XVI endorsed the use of condoms by those infected with HIV. This created much confusion among the laity, since it flew in the face of nearly one hundred years of Church teaching regarding contraception. This issue is too complicated to be dealt with in a footnote, but it *does* illustrate the confusion and suspicion that a conscientious American Catholic might have when dealing with issues like Freemasonry. It is puzzling to say the least, and reinforces the author's stance on the need for making decisions using an informed conscience. See Stacy Meichtry and Nathania Zevi, "Vatican Moves to Refine Pope's Views on Condoms," *The Wall Street Journal,* November 24, 2010, http://online.wsj.com/article/SB10001424052748704369304575632 484147228048.html. Web. 2010.

any religious course in life. If one wants religious instruction, one should go to a priest, rabbi, minister, or some other religious teacher. Masonry does not have a creed, or a doctrine for gaining eternal life. My advice is to go to a church if you are looking for such things.

As for the charges of devil worship, usually critics will pick out a Masonic writer from the past, and selectively quote him as an authority on Freemasonry. Brother Albert Pike is a favorite writer used by these detractors. Pike wrote prolifically in the Nineteenth Century about Masonic topics. Much of what he wrote deals with his personal musings on religion and philosophy. Antagonists will usually start by saying that Pike is "The Authority" on Freemasonry. Then they will quote a few lines out of context and "prove" that Freemasons worship Satan. One more time: there *is* no authority that speaks for Masonry! Quoting Pike or anyone else does not win an argument!

My own experience has shown that most of these fundamentalists, if you dig a little, believe that everyone but their own followers are headed for perdition. One evangelist sells a whole series of books and recordings dealing with religious topics. Once I looked up the list of what was for sale and what "good" Christians should beware of. The list was endless. Freemasons, Catholics, Jews, Muslims, Lutherans, Baptists, Hindus, Mormons, Buddhists—you name it—they were bad! The only group that one could safely belong to was the one headed by the evangelical leader—and don't forget to send a generous contribution to him and his "ministry."

Let me close by repeating once again that our oaths and obligations are symbolic only. The Candidate is told this at every step in the process of joining. They are traditional and serve to reinforce the solemnity of the occasion. Next, there is nothing wrong with taking an oath, *per se*. I've taken them when called for jury duty, when I've testified in court, when I joined the armed services, and when I took a job with the Federal Government. Most citizens take various oaths throughout their lives and don't feel that their souls are in danger. Masonic obligations are no different.

Conspiracy Charges

Believe it or not, there are even *more* extreme charges than devil worship made against the Fraternity. Some writers allege that Freemasons are part of a world-wide conspiracy that controls finance, governments, and all major institutions. Many writers have made a good living helping to spread this theory. One of the first, Leo Taxil, published his *Complete Revelation upon Freemasonry* in 1885 in France. This was the first of a series of books in which he claimed to "expose" the perils of the international Masonic conspiracy. He charged that Albert Pike was the "Pope" of the organization, that a congress had been held in Paris to plan world revolution, and that Freemasons practiced free sex and devil worship. He tendered his work to the Catholic Church and received payments and honors from the Vatican. It was somewhat embarrassing when he publicly admitted in 1895 that everything he had written was a pure fabrication.[73]

In the 1970's a British journalist, Steven Knight published a series of novels and non-fiction books in which he accused Freemasons in England of dominating the Home Office and the London Police. He also implicated Freemasons in one of his books in the "Jack the Ripper" murder case.[74]

---

[73] Coil, *Masonic Encyclopedia*, p. 647.
[74] Robinson, p. 305.

There *was* a financial scandal with Masonic overtones in Italy in the 1970's. A Masonic Lodge of Research named *Propaganda Due,* or P-2, was expelled by the Italian Grand Lodge and its warrant confiscated. The master of the lodge continued to hold meetings and converted it to his own purposes. He eventually used it to build a network of politicians, bankers, and publishers throughout Italy. Many members were implicated in a financial scandal involving banks closely allied to the Vatican. The story is too complex to relate here, but it involved embezzlement, murder, Cardinals, and hundreds of millions of missing dollars. Even though it was really a Vatican scandal, Freemasonry was also tarred as well.[75]

As with most conspiracy theories, one can never marshal enough facts to stay ahead of the charges. The truth simply doesn't matter at a certain point. For example, to this day one can buy a copy of a book entitled *Protocols of the Elders of Zion* which "proves" an international Jewish conspiracy that controls the world. The fact that the entire book was fabricated by the Russian Czar's secret police in 1903 doesn't matter to conspiracy mongers today. With the advent of the internet, it is literally impossible to combat new errors and conspiracy theories circulating around the globe. This will probably be a permanent problem for Freemasonry in the future.

Racism

Charges that Freemasonry is a racist organization really make some of the Brethren squirm. What makes me personally uncomfortable is that this charge has some basis in historical fact. Remember that Freemasonry can be defined as "The Brotherhood of Man, under the Fatherhood

---

[75] Ibid. pp. 313-317.

of God." All men who are of good character, believe in a Supreme Being, and can financially bear the burden, are eligible for membership. However, most lodges reflect the society in which they exist. For much of the history of Pennsylvania, informal segregation by race has been a fact of life. This has carried over into Masonic custom in our state. Most lodges have been overwhelmingly white. This situation was reflected all across the nation and compelled African American men to form segregated lodges if they wanted to become Freemasons.

In 1775, a freedman named Prince Hall and fourteen others were initiated in Irish Military Lodge No. 441 in Boston. The city was then under occupation by the British Army. Hall formed African Lodge No. 1 under the authority given him by this army lodge. This was a normal practice of the day. When English forces were driven out of Boston in 1776, Hall and his fellows attempted to join the established "regular" (white) lodges in the city. They were rejected—probably for racial reasons. Hall and his fellows secured a warrant from the Grand Lodge of England in 1784 that gave them the authority to form other lodges and even grand lodges. This was the Masonic legal basis for what came to be called "Prince Hall Masonry." In state after state, black men who wished to join the Fraternity had to enter the Brotherhood through these competing Grand Lodges. Even though they were lawfully organized under the authority of the Grand Lodge of England, they were treated as unlawful clandestine organizations by the "regular" Grand Lodges in each state.

In 1813, The Grand Lodge of England reorganized itself into the "United Grand Lodge of England." It also canceled many of the warrants that had been granted previously in years past. One of these warrants was the one for African Lodge No. 1. This eliminated the legitimacy of the lodge since no American Grand Lodge stepped in and recognized its members as Freemasons. In turn, all of the lodges and Grand Lodges across the United States that traced their warrants to it were, in turn, now considered illegitimate. The efforts of the Massachusetts Prince Hall Grand Lodge to regain its warrant, or to get recognition from the United Grand Lodge of England proved fruitless. So, from 1824 on, all black Masonic lodges were considered clandestine—or not really Masonic—by white Freemasons. For over two hundred years all state Grand Lodges had black counterparts. It was an alternate Masonic universe.[76]

Beginning in 1989, U.S. Grand Lodges began to recognize Prince Hall Grand Lodges. This involved a formal acceptance of Prince Hall Masons as legitimate, and extension of the right of mutual visitation to each other's members. What opened the floodgates was the acceptance of the Prince Hall Grand Lodge of Massachusetts by the United Grand Lodge of England in 1994. The Grand Lodge of England did not admit any mistakes in canceling the original 1784 warrant, but it did extend recognition. This "healing" of the warrant removed any legitimate reason by other American Grand Lodges for withholding Masonic recognition from Prince Hall Masons.

During the decade of the 1990's the movement to reach out to Prince Hall Grand Lodges steadily advanced. Despite some racial ugliness, the movement did not stop. The Grand Lodge of Pennsylvania voted to extend recognition in 1997. As of 2026, two Grand Lodges still have shamefully refused to accept the obvious and

---

[76] Roberts, *Freemasonry in American History,* pp. 261-263.

recognize black Freemasonry in some form. They are the Grand Lodges of South Carolina and Mississippi.[77] Louisiana and West Virginia recognize Prince Hall Masonry in another state, but not in their own jurisdictions. This appears to be a hybrid compromise that—while not perfect, at least shows *some* commitment to progress and change.

Until these Grand Lodges come to their senses and regularize their procedures, they will continue to provide evidence that critics can use to smear Freemasonry with the charge of racism.

"I bet you if I met him and had a chat with him, I'd find him a very interesting and human fellow because, you know, I really never met a man that I didn't like."

---Brother Will Rogers (referring to Russian leader Leon Trotsky).

---

[77] Coil, *Masonic Encyclopedia*, pp. 99-101. http://bessel.org/masrec/phamap.htm
http://Freemasons For Dummies, last modified 2/04/26

Famous American Brethren

Edwin "Buzz" Aldrin, Stephen F. Austin, "Count" Basie, Irving Berlin, **Daniel Boone**, Ernest Borgnine, Jim Bowie, Omar Bradley, William Jennings Bryan, Joshua L. Chamberlain, Henry Clay, Ty Cobb, William F. "Buffalo Bill" Cody, George M. Cohan, Nat "King" Cole, Samuel Colt, Jack Dempsey, William O. Douglas, Jimmy Doolittle, W.E. B. DuBois, "Duke" Ellington, Bob Evans, Bob Feller, Glenn Ford, Henry Ford, **Benjamin Franklin**, Clark Gable, John Glenn, Lionel Hampton, John Hancock, W.C. Handy, Patrick Henry, J. Edgar Hoover, Sam Houston, Jesse Jackson, Al Jolson, John Paul Jones, Francis Scott Key, the Marquis de Lafayette, John A. LeJeune, Lewis & Clark, Charles Lindbergh, Douglas MacArthur, **George Marshall**, Thurgood Marshall, Christy Mathewson, Willie Mays, **Andrew Mellon, Tom Mix,** Audie Murphy, Brad Paisley, **Arnold Palmer**, Norman Vincent Peale, J.C. Penny, John J. Pershing, Adam Clayton Powell, Richard Pryor, Charles Rangel, **Ed Rendell**, Paul Revere, Eddie Rickenbacker, Branch Rickey, "Sugar Ray" Robinson, Will Rogers, John Philip Sousa, Danny Thomas, Mark Twain, **Honus Wagner, "Pop" Warner**, Earl Warren, Booker T. Washington, John Wayne, Grant Wood, Cy Young,

(These are just a few of the most famous. Pennsylvanians are in boldface.)

EMBLEMATIC STRUCTURE OF FREEMASONRY

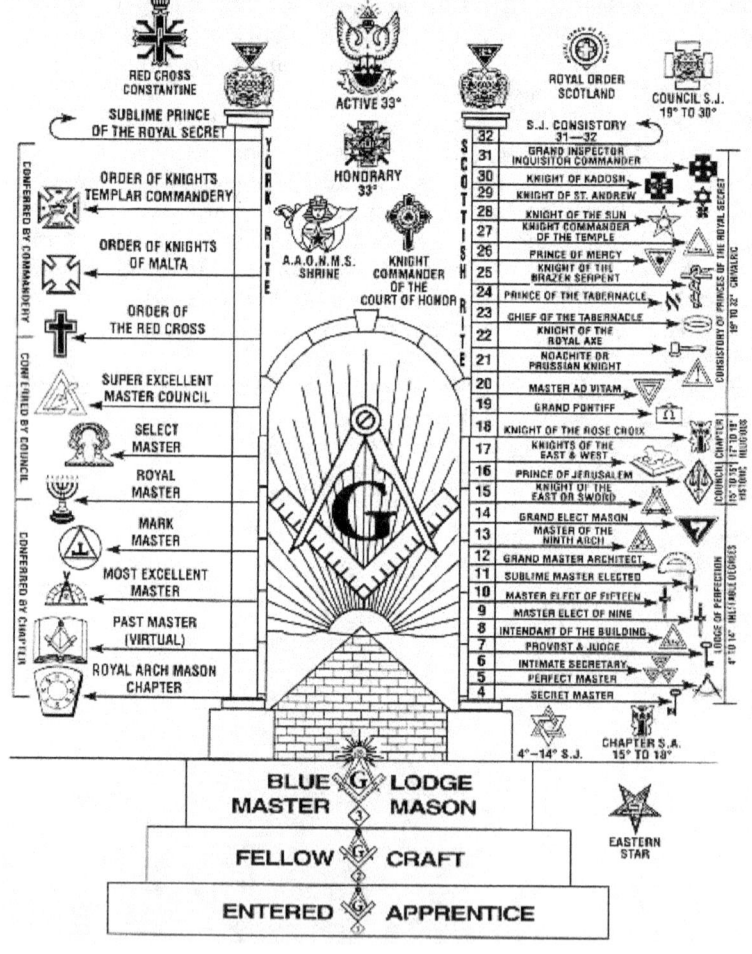

9. PERSONAL GROWTH AS A FREEMASON

As I've said before, personal growth in Masonry is up to the individual. It is up to *you* to decide what you want to do, or what kind of Mason you want to be. One can look at the Fraternity as an intellectual course of study, a school for self-improvement, or as a social club. There is room for all types of men in the lodge. You will probably hear the appellation "Knife and Fork Mason" used to describe some Brethren who seem to care most about the food served at lodge. Usually, it is meant as a joke or is used in a kindly manner.

There is nothing really very wrong with this orientation. Every man must choose his own Masonic path. Fellowship is an important part of the Masonic experience. Every man must get out of Masonry what he is capable of. Also, who can say if such attitudes don't contribute something very important to lodge life? All of us have different talents. Some have a talent for friendship and human warmth. We shouldn't denigrate such members. We need them.

This book earlier recommended getting involved in your lodge at any level in order to start your journey of Masonic discovery. This is still the best way in my opinion. As a new Freemason, don't feel rushed. Don't feel that you have to join every committee or volunteer for everything. Don't burn yourself out. Get involved, but don't overdo it.

Eventually, at your own pace, you may want to explore additional aspects of Freemasonry. The Fraternity has many other options to experience. They are called the "Appendant Orders." There are so many that a chart is useful in organizing them. If you look on page 126, you will see what I mean. It looks confusing, but bear with me, I will explain.

At the base is the so-called "Blue Lodge." The additional bodies are open only to Master Masons in good standing. One must start out as a regular Freemason in order to be considered for membership in any additional order. In Pennsylvania there are two major branches of Appendant bodies.

On the left is the older branch called "The York Rite." On the right is the branch called "The Scottish Rite." The York Rite grew out of Eighteenth-century Freemasonry. In fact, one of its Degrees, The Royal Arch, was conferred as early as the 1750's in America. The Scottish Rite originated in France in the 1700's and came to the United States in 1801. Both of these bodies are old and distinguished organizations. They both offer significant opportunities, but they are different in style, and in how they are organized.

Each of the two branches confer Degrees in a different manner, and each offers a different experience to their membership. Don't get the idea, however, that one is in any way superior to the other. Both simply have different goals, methods, and atmosphere.

We will begin with *The Scottish Rite.* This has become the most popular Appendant body in Pennsylvania over the years. It is also the group that has the 32 Degrees. It is probably one of the best known of the Masonic bodies.

The Scottish Rite is organized differently. It does not meet locally in lodges, but in a much larger body called a

"Valley." These Valleys cover wide areas of the state. They draw members from several surrounding Masonic Districts and have large buildings where they meet called "Scottish Rite Cathedrals." There are sixteen such Cathedrals in Pennsylvania. Also, Degrees are conferred twice a year during what are called "Reunions."

Degrees are much different than in the "Blue Lodge." First of all, there are usually dozens of Candidates for the Scottish Rite, sometimes many more. Reunions only last two days, so the Degree work must, of necessity, be on a mass scale. Degrees are conferred in the Cathedral's auditorium and all Candidates sit in the audience and watch the Degree performed onstage. Normally one Candidate is selected to "exemplify" the others. Degrees are presented in the form of plays, with dialogue and costumes. Some are very elaborate. Also, there is not enough time to present all 32 Degrees. About six or so are presented over the course of the two-day reunion. When I became a member years ago, I received the 4th, 14th, 16th, 17th, 18th, 20th, 26th, and the 32nd Degrees over the course of the weekend. The Degrees can be very entertaining and thought provoking, but regretfully individual participation has to be kept to a minimum.

Scottish Rite Cathedrals are very social in their orientation. They usually sponsor dinners, entertainment events, picnics, and outings for families.

Chapter   Council   Commandery

Next comes *The York Rite* of Freemasonry. The York Rite is mainly a continuation of the Degrees in the Masonic lodge. There are three bodies within the rite: the Royal Arch Chapter, the Council of Royal and Select Master Masons, and the Commandery of Knights Templar. A Candidate may join only one body, but normally he joins all three. It can take up to a year to progress through all the Degrees. Chapter and Council Degrees build on the Biblical story of the Temple of Solomon at Jerusalem and its eventual destruction. The Commandery is based on the historical warrior monks, the Knights Templar. It is also one of the bodies within Freemasonry that is strongly religious in character and only accepts Candidates who profess Christianity. It is, therefore, one of the exceptions to the rule of keeping religion out of Masonry. The Degrees are much like the ones conferred in the Blue Lodge. Usually there is only one Candidate, and he is the focus of the evening. York Rite bodies usually meet once a month in a fashion similar to Masonic lodges. They have their own officers and Degree nights. The ritualistic work of the three bodies would look somewhat familiar to a Master Mason and so would the Degrees, for the most part. There are nine degrees in

Pennsylvania York Rite Masonry, although no one goes around speaking of himself as a "Ninth Degree" York Mason.

Shriners International has the biggest public profile of all the Appendant Masonic bodies. They host the Shrine Circuses in cities all over America, they march in parades and, most importantly, they own the Shriners Hospitals for Children. The organization is even larger than the Scottish Rite. There are eight shrine headquarters around the State and they draw members from even larger areas around them. In order to join the Shrine, one must be a Master Mason in good standing at your local lodge. There are no additional qualifications.

The Shrine is dedicated to good works and helping children, but the organization is also devoted to fun and good fellowship. There are dinners, clubs, groups of all kinds to join, and family fun is stressed. The initiation is given *en mass* as in the Scottish Rite at a Ceremonial, usually held twice a year. It also resembles attending a play and there is one Candidate onstage who stands in for the entire class of entrants.

There are a couple of Appendant bodies that should be mentioned next: *The Grotto*, and *The Tall Cedars of Lebanon*. The Grotto is smaller than the Shrine but operates in much the same way by being dedicated to fun and good fellowship. Their initiation is somewhat similar to the Shrine's. The Tall Cedars of Lebanon is also oriented towards recreation. Both of these groups require only that a prospective member be a Master Mason.

The Order of the Eastern Star is unusual in Freemasonry in that it is a body that men *and* women can join. Indeed, it was invented in the Nineteenth Century in order to give women a chance to experience Masonry in some form. Many husbands and wives join so that they can share the Masonic experience together. A Chapter must be sponsored by a Masonic Lodge, but it is run by its female members.

   The Pennsylvania Lodge of Research was warranted by the Grand Lodge of Pennsylvania in the year 2000. It is dedicated to Masonic study and education. Applicants for membership must be Master Masons in good standing. It meets four times a year in various locations around the state. Papers, study projects and book presentations are usually part of the agenda. If you are academically inclined and wish to study Freemasonry in a serious way, this might be a body you might look into joining.
   There is also another academically-oriented organization available to Brethren in the Commonwealth: *The Pennsylvania Academy of Masonic Knowledge.* Warranted by the Grand Lodge, its goal is to provide an individual the opportunity to engage in a self-directed course of Masonic studies and to share that knowledge with other Brethren. It operates in a similar manner to remote-studies programs run by academic institutions. If you are so inclined, it can also be an excellent way to become not only a student of Masonry, but a published author, if such a thing appeals to you.[78]
   There are two other groups that I sincerely hope you, as a newly raised Master Mason, might consider joining. They will take some time and commitment, however. They also aren't for everyone, for not everyone attains membership. They aren't technically organized bodies in

---

[78] Web. Home - Academy of Masonic Knowledge (pamasonicacademy.org) 22/09/2022.

the recognized sense. If you see a brother wearing the silver jewel depicted below, thank him for his service.

This is the jewel of a *Past Worshipful Master*. It means that this Brother has served his lodge in the East for one year and is now retired from actively "going through the chairs." There is a lot of wisdom and experience symbolized by this ornament. Try and get to know such Brethren better.

Finally, my sincere wish for you is that you attain the *50-Year Membership* lapel pin. Think of such an achievement! It symbolizes all that is best in a man's life: wisdom, commitment, loyalty, perseverance, and a long, blessed life. I hope Brother, that you can attain this last Masonic honor.

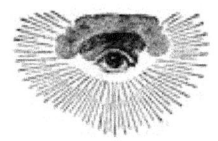

CLOSING
What Happens Now?

What happens now depends upon what *you* do. Like many aspects of life, individual commitment can determine whether you are satisfied with your Masonic choice. Many men join the Fraternity and, after a few months or years, decide that Masonry is little more than a glorified men's club, or an empty set of meaningless rituals. It can be, if you don't bother to actively look at what you are taking part in or try to understand its significance.

Rituals of all sorts are as old as human civilization. Ceremonies can be of several kinds. They can commemorate the dead, celebrate good luck, mark the seasons, or try to get us in touch with our higher purposes. Masonic ritual addresses all of these different aspects of human aspiration.

Modern life can become a battle for one's sanity. All day, every day, forces compete for our attention and energy. Family, children, job, taxes, wife, in-laws, parents, friends, politics, the list seems endless—and relentless. Sometimes it's hard to find a small space for oneself to breath. Freemasonry can give you that space Brother.

The lodge provides a quiet place where one can meet real friends who simply wish the pleasure of your company. Ritual can play a transforming effect on oneself, and on others. By taking on a role, or a different persona, we become "other." We lose ourselves in something larger. Masonic ritual gives its participants a vision of the good, the true, and the beautiful that remains in the soul even after we have returned to the chaos and confusion of our everyday lives. During the ceremony, something new comes alive within us. By submitting to the unique demands of ritual, we give ourselves up to a larger pattern and create—at least for that evening—a unity of time, space, heaven, earth, and of the eternal in all of us.[79]

How can you become jaded with such an opportunity as this? Attend lodge. Try to be useful in your lodge. Make an effort to learn and advance yourself in Masonic knowledge. If you are dissatisfied with your Brethren or their customs, respectfully and gently try to reform them. Remember your oaths and obligations to your fellows. Do what you can, where you can, when you can.

Let me close with a quote from Brother Francois Marie Arouet, sponsored by Benjamin Franklin, and initiated into the Lodge of the Nine Sisters in Paris, 1778. He is better known as the philosopher and writer Voltaire. In one of his novels, he has a character repeat this advice over and over: "We must cultivate our garden." [80] *That* is what should come next. Labor to build yourself into a better human. Cultivate your personal garden. Good luck Brother. I hope to meet you in Lodge.

[79] Karen Armstrong, *The Great Transformation: The Beginning of our Religious Traditions*, New York: Alfred A. Knopf, 2006, p. 76.
[80] Voltaire, *Candide*, New York: Bantam Books, 1971, p. 120.

AFTERWARD
Looking Back and Ahead

With age, I've become less reflective. I seldom revisit the books I've written. My philosophy has been to write as well as I can, support my conclusions with evidence, and set my work "free" to make its way in the world on its own. There is less stress that way. Recently however, I've been compelled to alter this practice. Due to advances in the technology used by my publisher, I was required to closely reexamine *A Pennsylvania Masonic Handbook.* I was forced to honestly look at, and judge, the book.

The *Handbook* was composed in 2009 and published in 2010. It was my first major foray into writing. I was curious as to how well it had aged. Was its message still valid? Would the older writer that I am now suggest major changes to its content? Were its conclusions wrong? Happily, I can answer that, even with all its faults, no major changes are needed.

The *Handbook* is not perfect. Its tone is somewhat *jejune* and "pollyannish." It could be more serious, but my counter is that it was not written for scholars of Freemasonry, but for the average new Brother who doesn't have the time or inclination for deep study. It is a "how to," and a "why" book, not an academic treatise. It offers paths for further study, but can stand alone as a guide to the new member. I judge it a success in this way.

Footnotes and documentation for positions I took were also examined to see if they are still valid. With a single exception, they are. In the 1980's, Cardinal Joseph Ratzinger, as head of the Office of the Sacred Congregation for the Doctrine of the Faith, wrote a statement that Roman Catholics who joined Freemasonry were in a grave state of sin and could not receive communion. This statement did not have the force of law, and did not change the plain reading of the *Catechism of the Catholic Church.* The question of whether Catholics can choose to become Freemasons appeared to be closed. However, after Cardinal Ratzinger was elected Pope Benedict XVI in 2005, he did not clarify the Church's official position vis-à-vis the Fraternity. It is still up to individual conscience, but the legal justification for men joining *has* been weakened. As I originally wrote, the whole issue is still a muddle.[81]

Aside from this small problem, I have no regrets about the book itself. One problem remains, however. In the book, I stated that there were no Masonic books written especially for Pennsylvania Freemasons. In academic terms, there was a "gap" in the literature. I am sorry to say that this situation has not been remedied in the last decade. For better or worse, this is still the only book of its kind. I look forward to the day when it has competitors.

As to the future, I am confident, but add a word of caution. Freemasonry will endure, but it may well look very different. It will continue to shrink. I predict that someday most counties in Pennsylvania will have only one lodge. While the group experience remains central to membership, the Craft will become much more individually-oriented. Self-improvement, study, and personal growth will become a greater part of the experience. I intend to explore this subject in future research. If you have gotten this far in the book, I offer my thanks and good wishes. May the "genius of Freemasonry" preside over your conduct and guide you always, Brother.

R.B. Little Rock, 2022.

---

[81] Christopher Hodapp, *Freemasons for Dummies,* Hoboken, NJ: John Wiley & Sons, Inc., 2013, pp. 70-71.

BIBLIOGRAPHY

Armstrong, Karen. *The Great Transformation: The Beginning of Our Religious Traditions*, New York: Alfred A. Knopf, 2006.

Broderick, Ed., Robert C. *The Catholic Encyclopedia*, New York: Thomas Nelson Publishers, 1987.

Bullock, Steven C. *Revolutionary Brotherhood: Freemasonry and the Transformation of the American Social Order, 1730-1840,* Chapel Hill, NC: University of North Carolina Press, 1996.

Catechism of the Catholic Church, The Vatican: 1994.

Coil, Henry Wilson, *A Comprehensive View of Freemasonry,* Richmond, VA: Macoy Publishing & Masonic Supply Co., Inc., 1998.

--------------. *Outlines of Freemasonry,* Kessinger Publishing Co. LLC, Kila, MT, 2008.

--------------. *Coil's Masonic Encyclopedia,* Richmond, VA: Macoy Publishing & Masonic Supply Co. Inc., 1995.

Flexner, James Thomas. *George Washington and the New Nation (1783-1793)*, New York: Little, Brown and Company, 1969.

Haywood, H.L. *The Great Teachings of Masonry,* Richmond, VA: Macoy Publishing & Supply Co. Inc., 1986.

Hodapp, Christopher. *Freemasons for Dummies,* Hoboken, NJ, John Wiley & Sons, 2013.

The Holy Bible, KJV, Wichita: Heirloom Bible Pub, 1988

Huss, Wayne A. *The Master Builders: A History of the Grand Lodge of Free and Accepted Masons of Pennsylvania, 3 Volumes,* Philadelphia, PA: Grand Lodge, F. & A.M. of Pennsylvania, 1986.

140

Jacob, Margaret C. *Living the Enlightenment: Freemasonry and Politics in Eighteenth-Century Europe*, Oxford: Oxford University Press, 1991.

Kuhn, Thomas S., *The Structure of Scientific Revolutions*, Chicago, IL: The University of Chicago Press, 1970.

The Little Masonic Library, Book I, Richmond, VA: Macoy Publishing & Supply Co., Inc., 1977.

M*h*b**e, or The Grand Lodge Door Open'd, facsimile edition, Kessinger Publishing Company, Kila, MT, 2006.

McCullough, David. *Truman*, New York: Simon & Schuster, 1992.

Pirsig, Robert M. *Zen and the Art of Motorcycle Maintenance: An Inquiry into Values,* New York: Bantam Books, 1976.

Ridley, Jasper. *The Freemasons: A History of the World's Most Powerful Secret Society,* New York: Arcade Publishing, 2001.

Roberts, Allen E., *The Craft and Its Symbols: Opening the Door to Masonic Symbolism,* Richmond, VA: Macoy Publishing and Masonic Supply Company, Inc., 1974.

---------------. *Freemasonry in American History*, Richmond, VA: Macoy Publishing & Masonic Supply Co. Inc., 1985.

Robinson, John J. *Born in Blood: The Lost Secrets of Freemasonry,* New York: M. Evans & Co.: 1989.

Scirocco, Alfonso. *Garibaldi, Citizen of the World: A Biography,* Princeton, NJ: Princeton University Press, 2007

Solomon, Maynard. *Mozart: A Life,* New York: HarperCollins Publishers, 1995.

Stevenson, David. *The Origins of Freemasonry,* Cambridge: Cambridge University Press, 1998.

Tolstoy, Leo. *War and Peace*, New Library, New York: 1968.

Voltaire, *Candide*, New York: Bantam Books, 1971.

Yates, Francis A. *The Rosicrucian Enlightenment,* New York, NY: Routledge, 1972.

--------------------. *The Art of Memory*, Chicago, IL: The University of Chicago Press, 1966.

INTERNET RESOURCES

Masonic Service Association of North America. "Membership Totals since 1924." MSA. Web, 2008. http://www.msana.com/msastats.asp.

U.S. Department of Commerce, U.S. Census Bureau. "Demographic Trends in the 20th Century: Census 2000 Special Reports." U.S. Census Bureau, 2002. Web. http://www.census.gov/prod/2002pubs/censr-4.pdf.

The Grand Lodge of PA. "Membership History." Web. 2010. http://www.pagrandlodge.org/gsecretary/membershiphist ory.html.

Masonic Poetry, 2006. http://www.masonic-poetry.org/poems/entapsng.htm.

http://bessel.org/masrec/phamap.htm

ARTICLES

"Father is Brother After Son Confers Degree," The Pennsylvania Freemason Vol. XLIX, November 2002, No. 4.

"Renaissance Q & A with the Grand Master," The Pennsylvania Freemason Vol. LVII, August 2010, No. 3.

Akst, Daniel. "America: Land of Loners," *The Wilson Quarterly,* Summer 2010, The Woodrow Wilson Center for Scholars, Washington, DC.

Cowell, Alan. "After 350 Years, Vatican Says Galileo was Right: It Moves," *The New York Times*, October 31, 1992.

Meichtry, Stacy and Nathanial Zevi, "Vatican Moves to Refine Pope's Views on Condoms," *The Wall Street Journal,* November 24, 2010.

Untitled pamphlet distributed by Committee on Masonic Education, Grand Lodge F. & A. M. of Pennsylvania. Authorized and Approved by the Right Worshipful Grand Master. Circa 1995.

IMAGES

Images from Free Masonic Clip Art. Web.
http://www.fraternalclipart.com
All other images, or diagrams, are by the author. Author's picture from a personal collection. Cover design by the author.

About the Author

Robert E. Burtt was born in Du Bois, PA. An alumnus of the University of Pittsburgh, he earned Bachelor's and Master's Degrees in Political Science, and a Master's Degree in Public Administration there. He is a veteran of the U.S. Navy and is retired from the U.S. Department of Homeland Security.

He was raised a Master Mason in Harmony Lodge No. 429, Zelienople, PA in 1995. He is a Past Master of Harmony Lodge. A member of Delta Royal Arch Chapter No. 170, New Castle, PA, he is Past High Priest. He also belongs to Hiram Council No. 45, Royal and Select Master Masons, where he is Past Thrice Illustrious Master. He was knighted in Lawrence Commandery No. 62 (since merged with Lorraine Commandery No. 87,) and is Past Eminent Commander.

Brother Burtt is also a Charter Member of the Pennsylvania Lodge of Research. He was certified a Master Masonic Scholar by the Pennsylvania Academy of Masonic Knowledge, sponsored by the Grand Lodge of Pennsylvania, in 2021.

Mr. Burtt is married to his wife, Grace and lives out-of-state. He owes most of what he has accomplished to her steadfast support.

"Remember always Brethren, that these solemn rites, of which you have been partakers, and your parts in them, are as binding on your consciences out of the lodge as within it. They are links in that chain made in life, for eternity."[82]

---From the Closing Charge.

---

[82] Untitled pamphlet distributed by Committee on Masonic Education, Grand Lodge F. & A. M. of Pennsylvania. Authorized and Approved by the Right Worshipful Grand Master. *circa* 1995.